Falling in Love, Staying in Love

How to build a strong lasting relationship

Malcolm Stern
with Su Bristow

PIATKUS

09345899₄

Copyright © 2004 by Malcolm Stern and Su Bristow

First published in Great Britain as
The Courage to Love in 1996 by Piatkus Books
Piatkus Books Ltd
5 Windmill Street, London W1T 2JA
email: info@piatkus.co.uk

This revised and updated edition published 2004 by Piatkus Books

The moral right of the authors has been asserted

A catalogue record for this book is available from the British Library

ISBN 0 7499 2504 3

Edited by Krystyna Mayer
Text design by Goldust Design

This book has been printed on paper manufactured with respect for the environment using wood from managed sustainable resources

Typeset by Palimpsest Book Production Limited, Polmont, Stirlingshire

Printed and bound in Great Britain by
William Clowes Ltd, Beccles, Suffolk

Acknowledgments

We would like to acknowledge the support and encouragement of Judy Piatkus, Gill Bailey and especially our project editors, Anna Crago and Isabelle Almeida. We would also like to thank the many people around whose stories the book has been woven.

From Malcolm: I want to honour and appreciate my wife, Amanda, whose wisdom is helping me find the courage to love. Our children, Michael and Alexandra, and my daughter Melissa have been ongoing teachers of spontaneity, joy and beauty.

Thanks also to my parents, Moe and Helen, who have always loved me unconditionally, and to the many friends and teachers who have shone their light on my path. I am eternally grateful to the thousands of people who have worked with me in therapy over the years, and shared the depths of their feelings. Out of these meetings, the concept of this book was born.

Su has been a constant and inspiring friend and co-creator. Her writing is deep and poetic, and has enabled me to share my work. I would not have been able to do so without her.

From Su: heartfelt thanks to my partner, Martin, for his unflagging support and enthusiasm, and to my children, Rosie and Tom. To Malcolm, my fellow traveller and dear friend, my gratitude and love.

Contents

Introduction

We all know what it is like to fall in love. Even if it has never actually happened to you, you've read the books, seen the films, heard the music. It is seen in the West as the best thing that can happen between two people. We all know, however, if we have been there, that that is not the end of the story.

When you are in love, you can feel more real and alive than ever before, but you can't stay there. Sooner or later the enchantment wears off and your critical faculties return. You wake up to the fact that you don't really know this other person with whom you have fallen into partnership. What happens next?

Making a new map

It is the beginning of a long journey. You have no choice about whether or not to set out on the road, for we are all linked with other people in one way or another, and if you engage with others you will inevitably run into difficulties. You do have a choice, however, about how far and how fast you want to travel. Our parents and grandparents gave us maps and guidelines, however incomplete and contradictory; since then the signposts have been moved and the landscape itself has changed. We are tackling new questions in our relationships these days. We want less compromise, more intimacy and more truth, partnerships in which neither person takes power, and neither gives it away. For this new country, we have to make new maps for ourselves.

Falling in Love is an attempt to make such a map. At the core of it is *The Courage to Love*, the book we wrote together in 1996.

For this new edition, it has been substantially revised and expanded. Throughout *Falling in Love* there are exercises that enable you to try out for yourself some of the techniques and skills you will need on your relationship journey. They are based on hard experience rather than on wishful thinking; not on how we think people should be, but on how we actually are. The experience we have drawn upon is our own and that of the thousands of people who have passed through Malcolm's workshops or been in therapy with him since the late 1970s.

From Malcolm comes the primary inspiration and the wealth of experience in the field of psychotherapy. Hereafter, 'I' refers to Malcolm. However, this is a joint creation, and it speaks for us both. Most of the writing is Su's, the stories are Malcolm's and the book has been created from a shared vision. Our orientation is heterosexual, and this is reflected in the way we write. However, we are dealing here with issues that are common to all human relationships. Having acknowledged some of our limitations, we hope that, at least some of the time, we will be able to move beyond them.

People come into therapy with their pain, rage, grief and guilt, and they ask the same questions again and again. Where did it go wrong? Why don't my relationships last? How can I learn to relate better? What happened to the love that was between us? In *Falling in Love* we look at some of the places where relationships go wrong, and at what getting them right might look like.

There are no prescriptions here, for each of us ultimately has to find our own way, but there are guidelines, and there are some signposts and some well-trodden roads. Apart from drawing on our own experience, we have also drawn upon the wisdom of people living in other times and other cultures, for one thing is certain: we need new role models for relationship in these changing times, and we have to find them for ourselves.

Why bother?

The journey of relationship is a long and perilous one, fraught with many disappointments, dead ends, frustration and pain. So why should we put ourselves through all that suffering? Why not choose, as more and more people do these days, to live alone, without close ties to anyone? Or why not do as many of our parents did – and as most of us still do to some extent – and compromise, treading softly around each other, trading passion for security?

The answer to this question has many layers. The surface layer is that it hurts to be alone. We all have needs for companionship, support, intimacy and shared experiences. In order to be alone, you must deny those needs. And when you are in relationship, you find that it also hurts to compromise. Deep in all of us there is a yearning to meet and be met, to let down the barriers and find union. It is fear, in one or other of its guises, that holds us back.

So, just as pain drives us to withdraw and put up barriers, it also drives us to keep trying. Here is the key to the second layer. Why bother with relationships? It is because, as living beings, we have an inbuilt urge to grow, to realise ourselves more fully. This is with us from birth until death, and resisting it causes us pain. Relating to others, especially on an intimate level, stimulates the process of growth like nothing else. Here is where we are challenged, made to confront our own bad habits and expand our horizons. Relationships provide us with an essential key to self-transformation precisely because they give us so much trouble. It is through our mistakes and disasters that we are forced to grow.

When we have agreements with those close to us that relationships can work in this way, they can become one of the most potent tools for transformation available in our times. How can this be? It is because within an intimate relationship, we can create a safe environment to explore all those parts of ourselves that have been stunted, stifled and buried since childhood. Moreover, we can go beyond that and open up the immense potential that is within us. If we are willing to undertake the whole journey with another, the potential for alchemy – the transmutation of lead into gold – is there.

Here is the key to yet another layer of potential in relationships; one that you get a glimpse of when you fall in love, and perhaps at a few other exceptional moments in your life. When you enter into partnership with another who is willing to embrace the same perspective, the same commitment to find a way through the tangle of fears and neuroses that prevent you from touching each other, then you can co-create magic. It is probably the most amazing adventure you can undertake.

In *Falling in Love* we take a look at some of the basic skills you need to equip yourself for this adventure. They are not particularly complicated, nor in any way esoteric. They involve willingness to change, commitment to stay with the process of change as it unfolds and the resolution to keep practising.

The quest for aliveness has become my life's work, and I believe that our relationships offer us a wonderful opportunity to confront in ourselves all that keeps us from it. My own commitment is to try to stay conscious in my relationships, to be willing to grow and change, and to let go of whatever no longer works well.

Throughout *Falling in Love* I use stories to illustrate the points being made and to show how the people I describe have found ways to make changes in their lives. They are all true; only names and some other details have been changed to preserve confidentiality. I have chosen to present them in this way because doing so provides a window into the lives and experience of other people at a level that you would ordinarily never see, except perhaps at rare moments with your closest friends.

You will find your own life mirrored here. As Jacob Moreno, the founder of Psychodrama, (a therapeutic discipline which uses action methods, role training and group dynamics to facilitate constructive change in the lives of participants), said, 'We are all more alike than we are different.' If you are moved by any of these stories, if they put you in touch with your own emotions or present you with new insights, they will have served their purpose. Take what speaks to you, and use it as you will.

The exercises

Scattered throughout *Falling in Love* are exercises to be tried out on your own or with your partner. You can choose to do as many or as few as you like, and do them in any order, although they are arranged here in a logical progression. My invitation to you is to have a go. If you are reading this book because you and your partner really do want to work on your relationship, what have you got to lose? If you're not in a relationship and have a sneaking suspicion that there might be a few things you still have to learn, try out the ones you can do on your own. Of course, you can read the book without turning the spotlight on yourself at all, but you'll get a lot more out of it if you do.

A FEW GROUND RULES

Before you start, there are some basic rules that you need to establish between you and your partner. These are as follows:

1. THE RELATIONSHIP 'CONTRACT'

This applies not just to doing these exercises, but also to the whole pattern of your lives together. It states that in any given encounter what you are aiming for is a 'win-win' situation. In other words, neither of you is trying to prove the other wrong, or come out on top, or have the last word. This isn't always easy, especially if there are deeply rooted problems between you that have grown over the years, but if you can't agree to this contract, don't do the exercises. Instead, you need outside help to work through your 'stuff'; a couples' counsellor or mediator of some sort. That is another story.

If you try to do exercises like these without truly wanting a win-win result, you will dig yourselves deeper into the mire. Remember, the whole point of being in a relationship is to enhance your life – and that means *both* your lives. The aim is to come through to a place where you can have good times together, and not spend too much time analysing your relationship and reading books like this! Win–win means exactly what it says; both of you get what you really want out of it.

2. TIME AND PLACE

The second ground rule is about how and where you do the exercises. Choose your time and place with care; these exercises are about honouring your relationship and trying to take it deeper, so do it as if you mean it. Choose a time when you are not too tired, too stressed or upset; it's no good trying to sort all this out when you're in the middle of a flaming row. Make sure you won't be disturbed by children, phone calls or anything else.

Drinking a little alcohol before the exercises is fine, but you shouldn't be drunk or stoned, or hungry for that matter (low blood sugar can play havoc with your ability to think straight!). Decide in advance how long you will give it, and have in mind what you will move into afterwards, even if it's only going to bed; it can be very important to put boundaries on this type of intense focusing.

Choose your place carefully, too. If it is your normal living room, make it special by tidying up, covering up the television or computer, and maybe lighting candles – whatever it takes to turn it into a temple for this time. Have fun with it; if you could create the ideal place to hold your relationship, what would it look like? Try out different things at different times, but always be comfortable.

3. ACTIVE LISTENING

The third rule is to listen to your partner with full attention while they are speaking. Listen with your heart; don't judge, plan what you'll say in response or get caught up in your own reactions to what you're hearing. This is not your time. Don't interrupt, even to agree. If you like, you can have a 'speaking object', which could be anything from a stone or an ornament to a favourite stuffed toy. Whoever holds the speaking object can speak, and the other – or others – will listen.

Active listening is an art in itself, and essential for learning if you want to succeed in relationships, because a great deal of healing takes place simply in the process of being heard. If you truly feel heard by your partner, you become calmer and stronger; you don't have to strive for attention. The issue you're talking about may not get resolved – a lot of relationship issues are not really resolvable anyway – but the act of hearing and being heard is an act of true intimacy, and intimacy is what you are after. If you achieve it, the hunger to sort things out grows less, because sorting things out is only a step towards intimacy.

4. THANK EACH OTHER

The fourth rule, when each of you has taken your turn to speak and be heard, is to find a way to thank each other. You can do this with a hug, some eye contact and the spoken or unspoken message that you love and respect each other. If you've been moved by what your partner has said, let them know. If you have realised how you've been helping to create distance between you, acknowledge it. Do not, however, get into a big discussion. There should be no justifying and no explaining – that would only start another cycle of conflict. Leave it at that, and move on.

5. LET GO AND MOVE ON

A huge part of the art of relationships is learning to let go of things. Wanting to be right, wanting to win, is death to good relating, as we have seen. Speak with passion, listen with love, then let it go. The issue on which you disagree may come up again; that doesn't matter. Part of building trust and safety is learning that after going into sensitive areas like this, you will come together in love. Letting skeletons out of the closet will bring you closer, not divide you. So the fifth rule is that at the end of an exercise, you will step away from it.

6. DON'T BETRAY CONFIDENCES

The sixth rule is a big one. Whatever is said or done during these exercises is confidential, which means that unless the other person gives their permission you do not talk about what goes on to anyone else. This is essential if you are to build an atmosphere of trust and safety. In a group of friends, a lot of gossip goes around. Most of it is harmless, but it can be undermining, and if your friend or your partner has talked to you about sensitive issues, they need to know that it will go no further.

7. TAKE IT EASY!

The seventh and final rule is to take it lightly. This may sound ridiculous when you are struggling with really tough stuff – and relating is one of the hardest things we try to do – but somehow, you need to keep a sense of perspective. Remember that you are aiming for a good relationship at the end of it all, and part of a good relationship is knowing its limits. As Lebanese poet, philosopher and artist Kahlil Gibran said in *The Prophet*, 'Let there be spaces in your togetherness'.

Bring laughter into your interactions; entertain each other. Watch sitcoms together. The trials of partnership are one of the staples of comedy. This doesn't belittle the agonies and the dreariness that you may encounter, but it is a wise and creative way to do some healing.

Chapter 1
Falling in Love

**It does not much signify whom one marries
as one is sure to find next morning that it is
someone else.**

Samuel Rogers, English poet, 1763–1855

In the beginning . . .

Relationships begin with falling in love. This, at least, is the
expectation that we grow up with. You'll explore a little, go out
with a few girls or boys, and sooner or later the magic will
happen. That's how you'll know that this is the one for you,
the one with whom everything is possible. Perfect sex, no more
loneliness. Through the mists of 'happily ever after' can be
glimpsed the beautiful wedding, the shared home, the children.
You see yourselves caring for each other, growing old together,
knowing your place in the world because you have this one,
intimate, no-holds-barred relationship where you love, and are
loved, without reservation.

How many people do you know who actually do live happily
ever after? Take a look at your own relationships. Look at your
friends, your parents, the rich and the famous whose stories
scream for attention from every magazine stand. Which are the
ones that survive the difficult times, and which come to grief?

The plain truth is that the way a relationship begins, however much in love the happy couple may be, is a pretty poor predictor of its long-term prospects. An arranged marriage is more likely to last, in fact. What we do know for certain is that the state of being 'in love' does not last. Sooner or later, the passion begins to subside and the magic wears off. What happens next? And if romantic love is not really about making relationships, then what is it about?

In this chapter we take a look at what the real meaning of romantic love may be, and what you can learn from it – about yourself, and about the people you choose as partners. What is being in love actually like? If it isn't a good doorway to relationship, what is the point of it? The journey begins with your own experience; only after a close look at yourself can you move on to consider the Other, the object of your love. How do you choose, and what does your choice have to show you? Through becoming more aware and awake, how can you make the most of being in love, whether you take it forwards into a relationship or not?

A love story: Mick and Anna

Mick and Anna first met by phone, after a mutual friend decided to play matchmaker. Their conversation went well; they were both ready to find the other attractive and it was exciting to play with possibilities in this way. The next step was to exchange letters, and Mick describes how 'Anna wrote one and a half pages, very elegant and precise. I loved her writing and the way she expressed herself.' He laughs. 'I replied with thirty-six pages of drivel. I just poured it all out! She liked that, too, my spontaneity and openness.' By the time they were actually able to meet face to face, they were already well on the way to falling in love.

Their first meeting more than fulfilled their hopes and expectations. They began a very passionate affair, and after a couple of months Mick moved into Anna's house. There is a kind of selective blindness about falling in love; you simply ignore or dismiss any potential problems. It is the most powerful spin factory on Earth. Your differences get fed into the mutual admiration machine instead of being stumbling blocks. Anna thus enjoyed Mick's ability to flow with his feelings, while Mick loved her ability to condense, to analyse what she felt and express it clearly and economically.

Would you be surprised to hear that it was these differing qualities that led to their break-up? As the first intensity of the love between them began to wane, they settled into partnership. What brought them to grief, as so often happens, was the way they handled conflict. After an argument Anna would want to talk about what had happened, to try to understand how they had got into difficulties, resolve any hurt feelings and learn from the experience. Mick's way of dealing with arguments, on the other hand, was to let go of the emotional tangle and move on, meeting each new situation afresh.

Anna and Mick both began to be frustrated by the attitude of the other. Anna felt that Mick was avoiding the issues between them and trying to bury any unpleasantness under the carpet. Mick felt that she was simply giving the conflict fresh energy, dwelling on things that were better forgotten, and sabotaging what was happening in the present.

Anna and Mick could not find a way to resolve the problem. It became a huge issue between them, and what they had formerly admired in each other now became hateful. Mick saw Anna as obsessive, neurotic, endlessly wanting to pick things to pieces and unable simply to be. Anna was enraged by what she saw as Mick's refusal to deal with trouble – his avoidance of responsibility and rejection of opportunities to deepen their intimacy. By a slow and painful road they came to the point where they felt that they could no longer live together in love, so they split up.

Anna and Mick's story has a lot of things to show us. It begins with what I often think must be the ultimate con-trick, the way in which romantic love alters your perceptions so that everything about your beloved seems delightful – often to the horror of your friends, who can't borrow the rose-coloured spectacles.

Mick and Anna were the same people at their parting as they had been when they met. Held by the transcending power of love, they had moved into deep intimacy, and all the potential barriers to union had simply dissolved away. This place is no illusion. When you are there, you can feel more intensely real and alive than ever before. But you can't stay there. Sooner or later you fall back into yourself. If the tide of love has swept you into partnership, into living with another, perhaps having children or working together, then you have to learn how to engage on the everyday level as well, day by day, task by task, misunderstanding by misunderstanding.

Here is where a relationship truly begins. Here is where you need to muster all the skills at your command and start to learn new ones. You need to find support. You need to forgive your partner, and yourself, for being human.

Sometimes, of course, it becomes blindingly obvious as the glamour drops away that there is no chance of developing a partnership. More often, however, things are not so cut and dried. Mick and Anna chose to split up, but I believe that if they had wanted to they could have found a way through. This is where support from others is so essential, so that when you get stuck in head-on confrontation, as they did, someone else is available to offer a new perspective, another way of looking at things. There is always another way.

Exercise 1
How do my friends see me?

This is a useful exercise to do when you and your partner are stumbling over issues like these – but do it *before* you get to the point where you hate each other!

Each of you needs to find five friends willing to play the game. They should be people you can trust, who will not give you false praise, but won't tear you apart either. Choose wisely!

STEP 1

Meet with these five friends one by one, and ask them to give you honest and loving feedback about how they see you. If necessary, some of the meetings could be by phone or even email, but try to make most of them face to face. Here are the questions to ask:

What do you particularly like about me? What do you see as my strengths?

What do you find difficult about me? What do you see as my weaknesses?

What does everyone think about me?

While your friends are talking, just listen. Afterwards, thank them, but do not start to analyse what they said or defend yourself. If any of these friends is up for it, you can return the favour by answering their questions in turn. Remember: this is not about picking your friendship to pieces. It is about getting honest reflections of yourself that you can work on.

STEP 2

Get together with your partner in private at a time and place where you both feel comfortable and you will not be disturbed. Take it in turns to talk about what your friends have said – especially about the more difficult points. So, for example, you might say, 'X says he finds it really annoying that I'm always late when we arrange to meet.' Only talk about yourself, not about your partner. Your partner will listen, and thank you, but will make no other comment. This is not about scoring points off each other!

If it goes well, and you both try for honesty, you will learn a lot. Normally, when your partner nags you about untidiness, or spending too much money, or whatever else they find diffi-cult about you, you can ignore them, get defensive, or go on the attack with complaints of your own about them. But if two or three of your friends have also picked up on the same issues, maybe you really do have a problem. Take a look at it. Whatever it is, however trivial it may seem to you, it is getting in the way of your closest relationships. Do you really want that? Maybe you can do something about it.

Your partner, meanwhile, will hear his or her own concerns about you mirrored in what your friends say. This can be a huge relief; to know that others feel it too means that you are not neurotic or unreasonable, that you are not alone. And because your partner is hearing you admit these things yourself, face to face, and then doing the same thing in return, there are no points to be scored. Neither of you is perfect, but neither of you is alone and friendless either. Along with the less pleasant feedback will come some really positive comments that will surprise and delight you. Make sure you take those on board as well.

In saying this, I do not want to imply that it is necessarily better to try to make a relationship work. In a lot of ways, falling in love is an end in itself. You have the choice, then, whether to explore your relationship or not. Doing so offers you the opportunity – it opens a door that you might otherwise be too scared to open for yourself.

What lies beyond that door is the subject matter of the rest of this book. For now I want to focus on what being in love means to you as an individual, not as a way of engaging with another person, but as an experience in itself. If you can disentangle yourself from your preoccupation with the beloved, the state of being in love has some valuable insights to offer.

The love experience

Falling in love is an immensely powerful process; it could be the strongest emotional experience of your entire life. To be in love is to step into an altered state of consciousness, better than anything drugs or alcohol can do for you. You feel intensely alive, aware of your connections with the world around you, and full of wonder at its beauty. The barriers are down, your separateness is lost, and through union with the beloved, you feel complete, no longer alone.

A person who is in love has moved the centre of their being so that it now lies between the lover and the beloved. Such a person is in a state of ecstasy, a word whose root comes from the Greek *ex-stasis*, or standing outside oneself.

Human beings have a deep need to experience ecstasy, and in the past we have most often found our way there in a spiritual or religious context. It is no accident that people often describe being in love in mystical or spiritual terms. It seems that as the place of ecstatic experience at the heart of spiritual life has been lost or suppressed, so its place in the realm of relationships – in romantic love – has become much more important to us. We have a longing to stand outside ourselves, to lose our separateness and to merge with the divine, and this longing will find expression in one way or another. If the path of spirit is not open to us, it will seek us out wherever we are most vulnerable, wherever the walls of our personal castles can be breached. Hence, when we fall in love, we encounter the divine indirectly.

Romantic love: the peak experience?

It's hardly surprising, then, that we place enormous emphasis on falling in love. In the relationship stakes, this is seen as the peak experience, and for its sake we will justify huge upheavals in our lives; leaving established relationships, moving house or changing jobs, becoming estranged from parents and families.

One client of mine left her husband and two young children, in secure financial circumstances, to live with a man who turned out to be frequently drunk and physically abusive. Even after she had more than once felt that her life itself was in danger, it was almost two years before she finally left him. When I asked her what it was that she saw in this man, she smiled wryly and said, 'He wrote poetry. I thought it was wonderful.'

The need to be with the beloved can be so imperative that it overrides everything else. If you cannot or do not choose to go with it, you suffer intensely. It also makes you horribly vulnerable. Your happiness now depends on the actions and responses of another person, and alongside the blissfulness of being in love

7

lie the torments of jealousy, the agony of not being loved in return and the heartache of separation. If this is where you feel most alive, then it is also where you may suffer the most intense pain.

What is really going on?

This leads back to the question of what romantic love has to offer you in terms of relationship. It is certainly not a way of ensuring that you live happily ever after, unless you are exceptionally lucky. Being in love requires a temporary suspension of critical faculties. The qualities that you see – or imagine you see – in another person, that lead you into falling in love with them, may be quite different from those needed to sustain a mature relationship. In addition, more often than not what you are seeing has more to do with your own projections than with the reality of another human being. This is the next area that we need to explore.

'The course of true love . . .'

Do you really think your beloved is someone you could spend your life with? When you're in the thick of it, it's hard to accept that you may have fallen in love with your own fantasies, but let's take a closer look.

Think about the circumstances in which you fall in love. For one thing, you don't tend to fall in love with people whom you already know well. There is a glamour about the beloved, a sense of mystery and potential, that does not sit well with old acquaintance. The mundane realities of the lives of people you already know tend to get in the way of the love experience rather than being an integral part of it, and this in itself might alert you – if you were not so deeply in love – to what is really going on.

Likewise, there is the apparent paradox that romantic love has a way of lasting longer if it is not consummated, or not returned. Such situations can include loving someone who cannot or will not return that love; loving without being sexual, in the way of old-fashioned courtship or the medieval tradition; or loving with limits of a different sort, as in a long-term affair in which the lovers choose not to live together because of other commitments. The ecstasy can be prolonged for many years or even for a life-time when it is not taken into full-blown, everyday relationship. Some of the greatest creative works have been produced by poets, writers, painters, and so on, in such a state of grace.

Some of the worst 'crimes of passion' have also been committed by people in the throes of romantic love. If you needed any more proof that this sort of love has little or nothing to do with the real person who is the target of it, think about the kind of behaviour it can inspire. At best, a lover will find excuses to get close to the beloved, whether or not their attentions are welcome. They may write letters, make phone calls, do some detective work. Sounds familiar? It's harmless enough, but at worst it becomes obsessive, and can involve stalking, harassing, threatening and, at the furthest extreme, being violent. The joke nowadays is that you know you've arrived as a celebrity when you acquire a stalker – because, of course, the rich and beautiful and famous are ideal targets for this sort of fantasy love.

The songs are full of stories about lovers who murder their beloved because he or she turns out to have other plans, which don't involve dancing to someone else's tune. At this end of the spectrum it becomes blindingly obvious that 'love', as in care and respect and so forth, has nothing to do with what is going on. Strip off the romantic packaging and what you see is the need to make the beloved your own; a hunger for control that will ride roughshod over the beloved's own needs and desires.

What happens, on the other hand, when there are no barriers in the way, and you are free to explore your passion to its fullest extent? I love you, you love me, all we want to do is be together all the time. In my own experience the state of being in love lasts for anything from six weeks to six months – perhaps longer if there is some constraint, such as not meeting very often. After that, little by little, the glamour wears thin and reality begins to show through. Your projections are brought home to roost, the goddess or the god departs. What then?

Through the looking-glass

If romantic love is largely a process of projection, then it might pay to take a good look at what you are projecting. What is it that you admire in the beloved, that you need to recognise or develop in yourself? Much has been written about the way in which a man may project his inner feminine qualities, or a woman her masculine qualities, onto a loved one, and what an excellent opportunity this can be to bring these parts of ourselves into consciousness. The process of projection, however, goes much further and deeper than that.

One thing is very clear: you don't fall in love by accident or at random. In theory, almost any two people can form a relationship, but we do not choose just anyone. Even when romance blossoms from nothing more than a moment of eye contact across a crowded room, you sense far more in that brief glimpse than you can possibly know. Neuro Linguistic Programming (NLP), a highly sophisticated modern therapeutic technique, teaches that 93 per cent of communication takes place without words. As you gazed into the eyes of your beloved, did you ever have the feeling that somehow you had known this person all your life? At one level this is nothing more nor less than the truth.

Exercise 2
Who is your beloved?

No one wants to do this sort of exercise when they are madly in love. The time to do it is when you are beginning to move beyond that stage; you still have intense feelings for your beloved, but you have begun to notice things that you find less than perfect. It is useful to do it, too, if your partner accuses you of wanting to control them or take them over, if they feel swamped or stifled in the relationship – and this can happen at any stage.

STEP 1

Sit quietly by yourself and think about your partner or your loved one. What qualities do you admire in them, and what do you find less lovable? List them in two columns, under your partner's name.

Now draw a circle, with a straight line dividing it into two halves, above and below. In the middle, at the centre of the line, write your own name. One by one, look at the things you listed, both 'good' and 'bad', and see where they fit into your circle. Are they qualities that you recognise in yourself? If they are, and you see them as good qualities, put them in the upper half of the circle. This is where your 'best self' lives, the self you want the world to see.

Now look at the 'bad' things. Be honest; is there some way in which, by seeing that quality in your partner, you are avoiding seeing it in yourself? For example, if they lose their temper easily, maybe you react by bottling up your anger. That way you get to be the saintly one! If this rings any bells, put those qualities in the lower half of the circle. This is your 'shadow self', the parts of you you'd rather not own. One way of dealing with them is to project them onto your nearest and dearest. It doesn't make for an easy relationship, of course, but we all do it to some extent. The more you can acknowledge and accept these qualities as your own, the more you lift the burden of carrying them from your partner, and the more you become free to enjoy yourselves together.

There should be some items left over. Put the 'good' ones outside and above your circle. These are things you'd like to own in yourself, but don't feel are a part of you. This list might include things like good looks, high intelligence, making people laugh – it's different for everyone. You've chosen a partner, or potential partner, who has those qualities, because you admire them and feel that somehow, if this person becomes your beloved, you will get to own them in your own life.

Guess what? It isn't going to work. As the relationship progresses, those qualities you don't see in yourself, however lovely, will become a stumbling block. If she's beautiful, what does that make you? If he's got a great sense of humour, what have you got? If she's clever, are you stupid? Rather than allowing you both to expand, the relationship then pushes you both into smaller circles that don't do you justice. Those qualities are the ones you need to work on bringing into your own picture of yourself; you should not try to acquire them by proxy. There is more about this in Chapter 4, on self-esteem (*see page 60*).

That leaves the 'bad' qualities you didn't sense in yourself at all. Look at them again. If they still ring no bells, check back to the first exercise. If these qualities really do belong to your partner it's likely that their friends would have picked up on them. If they didn't, think again.

There are three possibilities. The first – and this is the most likely one – is that you are lying to yourself about not owning this one. Ask yourself why you might want to do that and see what comes up. You could also talk this over with your friends: do they see this in you? The second is that you really are seeing something in your partner that nobody else has seen. Can this be true – and if it is, what does this mean for your relationship? The third possibility is that you are ascribing something to your partner that simply doesn't belong to them; to put it bluntly, you are making it up. Why would you do that? And again, what does this say about the health of your relationship? By the way, it's quite unlikely that you really are making things up about your partner. Even if you don't recognise it at all, the first possibility is most probably at work here, and these are projections of your own. As you work on yourself and your relationship, they will emerge from the shadows. Paul's story (*see page 13*) illustrates one way to identify them and call them home.

STEP 2

Come together with your partner at a quiet time that suits you both. Take turns to look at each other's lists and drawings. They will be a rich source of insights into yourself and into each other. Remember to thank each other afterwards; this is a great gift you have given. Releasing your partner from these projections does not weaken the relationship. It frees you both to see, and to love, with clear eyes.

You choose those who mirror you, those who will show you what you may be or may become; and all projections have some anchor in the reality of the Other. Hidden within the beautiful flower of love and passion, the unconditional adoration that blooms in the first stages of romantic love, is the recognition of all sorts of other qualities in the loved one, some of which are anything but adorable.

As you move through your relationships, and particularly if you explore intimacy with several partners along the way, you won't be able to help noticing that patterns emerge; the same issues come up time and time again, even when the new beloved seems at first to be completely different from the one before. This is because the work of relationship is soul work, and until you take up the challenge of self-transformation it will continue to present itself to you however hard you try to find an easier path.

The story that follows is an excellent illustration of how you can project qualities from your shadow self onto your beloved. Normally, you'd be too much in love to think about analysing what you were doing – but as Paul discovered, the rewards for doing this can be rich.

Paul was in his mid-thirties, and had been working on himself, in therapy and in other ways, for about eighteen months. He was much more in touch with his feelings than ever before, and felt that his life was opening up to all sorts of new possibilities. Perhaps not surprisingly, in the last few months he had fallen in love. The problem was that he had fallen in love with a woman, Sophie, who was already in a relationship, and she had made it clear that this was where she wanted to stay. As a relationship with her was out of the question, Paul's energies were channelled into intense self-examination. He had a fair understanding of where his feelings were coming from, but it made no difference to the strength of his obsession – his own word – so he brought it to therapy to try to gain some new insights.

We began by looking at what it was about Sophie that Paul found so powerfully attractive. She was certainly beautiful, and was putting out strong sexual messages that had, in the time Paul had known her, drawn a number of men into her orbit besides Paul himself. However, as Paul explored his feelings, it became clear that the sexual attraction was not the primary factor for him.

What had really moved him was his sense of Sophie's vulnerability. 'She's well defended, but she's very vulnerable inside, and she sometimes has trouble making decisions or knowing what she really feels, and that really hooks me. I just want to hold her and protect her. It melts me inside.'

Paul needed no prompting to recognise that it was something of his own that he was responding to here, but he was finding it difficult to call the projection home. His own vulnerability was irritating to him, a source of shame, and he readily admitted that this had been the attitude of his parents towards his insecurities as a young child. 'It's really hard to take that part of me seriously, or even to give it a voice at all. I tend to discount it automatically.'

Whom do we love?

This is a key point about projections, and one that explains much of their power. It is those parts of yourself that you discount automatically, that you don't even give a voice to, that tend to emerge in this form. So it comes about, at least in Western culture, that women often admire men who manifest power in some way – men who display the ability to achieve things in the world, to be single-minded, to 'be someone'. Men in turn are attracted to softness, vulnerability, fragility – precisely the qualities that Paul saw in Sophie. These are stereotypes, and we laugh at them when we recognise them, but they still influence our actions. As long as girls learn that it is not acceptable for them to be too powerful, and as long as boys learn that they must not show – or even feel – their feelings, we will continue to look to each other to do it for us.

There is not even an equal balance here, for we live in a patriarchal society that values the qualities it sees as 'masculine' above those it sees as 'feminine', and thus prizes achievement (on its terms) far more than knowing your own heart. Girls also learn that, although feeling is the province of the feminine, it is essentially weak, something to be ashamed of. They also learn to hide, even from themselves. We are therefore all touched when we find vulnerability in others; we are all attracted to people who seem more vividly alive than we do ourselves. Our drama and our literature are largely concerned with the exploration of emotions, pain and joy intensely felt and lived, at a safe distance from our everyday lives.

How can we begin to own these qualities in ourselves and to live them in our lives, rather than requiring other people to carry them for us? It is not enough, as Paul had discovered, to understand what we are doing. Paul knew all about how projection works and had been trying to apply this knowledge to himself, but it had made not a scrap of difference to the strength of his feelings. Understanding is fine as far as it goes, but the power of love arises in a different dimension of your being, one that is not in the least impressed by reason and analysis. In order to bring home these lost or potential parts of yourself, you have to allow yourself to experience them, to care for them, to bestow love where it rightfully belongs. In Paul's case, he had to allow *himself* to be vulnerable.

As we worked together, it became plain that it was no accident that Paul had fallen in love at this time and in this way. As a younger man, he had refused to admit to any kind of vulnerability, but he was now ready to reclaim it. He saw it as belonging to a much younger self, unsure and 'very childish, really', and at first it was very hard for him to take it seriously. Instead of owning it in himself, he was projecting it onto Sophie, where he could find it lovable without being ashamed.

Before Paul could really allow himself to hear the voice of his own younger self, he needed to take the time to focus on his feelings towards Sophie and to gain some clarity about what was going on there. I asked Paul to put himself into Sophie's position, and to speak as though he were Sophie addressing Paul. Immediately, without stopping to think through what he wanted to say, Paul-as-Sophie responded with, 'It feels as though you want to own me.' This came with the force of true insight. As I watched him, I saw the change; his eyes lit up and his presence – there is no simpler way to describe it – in the room grew stronger.

Once Paul was able to *experience* what was true for him in his heart and in his body, rather than trying to think his way into it, a shift became possible. When he tried speaking to his own younger self again, the difference was immediately obvious. The impatience and embarrassment he had felt earlier was gone, and in its place was a new tenderness and a readiness to listen. 'I can see it's really hard for you,' he said. 'I haven't given you much space, and I don't always hear you very well, but I'll give it a go.'

We finished the session by finding some very specific things that Paul could do, within the next week, to look after his younger self and let him out to play a little. After some hesitation, he said, 'I'll take him swimming next week. And I'll buy him an ice cream. How's that?'

These small commitments are very important; they mark the beginning of new habits, bringing them into reality in a down-to-earth way. When you are dealing with childlike and vulnerable parts of yourself, it is essential to keep your promises. For Paul, this was a first step in reparenting himself, in beginning to allow this and other unexpressed parts of his personality their rightful place in his life, to enable him to live his potential more fully. I would predict that as he continued to work on this – it might feel like work to start with – his obsession with Sophie would begin to fade. In nourishing the part of himself that called to him so strongly, he would no longer need to project it onto the outer world, and his love could be bestowed where it was truly needed.

Where do we go from here?

We have looked at what falling in love has to offer you as an individual, quite apart from the possibility of relationship. We have seen how it offers you the opportunity to know yourself better, through the recognition of your own projections. Once you can see them and own them, you can begin the work of filling your own holes, of living more of your potential, rather than looking for someone else to do it for you.

It is at this point that you begin to be capable of real relationships. When the enchantment of romantic love is at its height, it may feel as though you have found your soulmate, your 'other half', but this is an illusion. You can't even see the other person through the dazzle. Relating only becomes possible when the spell wears off. And when it does wear off, you have some profound choices to make.

What then?

You stand face to face with another human being – a stranger, someone with needs and expectations of their own, which may or may not dovetail with yours; someone equally bewildered, disappointed or angry that you are not what you seemed to be. It is no one's fault, but blame hangs in the air. The old defences spring back into place, sharpened by dismay that you have made yourself so vulnerable, revealed so much. Maybe you've made promises to this person, sacrificed people or things that you hold dear. What do you do now?

The possibilities that lie ahead are limited only by your own fears and conditioning. You can leave, say goodbye. You can say that it was wonderful for a while, but you weren't right for each other after all; maybe next time would be better. There is grief and hurt in this, especially when one partner still wants to make a relationship work, but it is as clear-cut as relationship ever gets, and it leaves you free to fall in love again. Like the other roads to ecstasy, love can be addictive. The myth is very persuasive; if love departs, it must mean that this was the wrong person after all. Somewhere out there, the ideal partner is still waiting . . .

Alternatively, you can stay physically and leave emotionally, to a greater or lesser degree, hoping – although usually this is not consciously thought through – to cause the minimum of pain and disruption, meeting some of your relationship needs and denying the rest. Most of us have tried this at some stage, and if the other person agrees to play the game the foundations are laid for a long-term, stable partnership. If you don't engage emotionally, you don't rock the boat. Many a marriage works like this, with large areas of compromise and a tacit understanding that tricky areas will be avoided.

Quite a few of us inherit this sort of model from our parents, to a greater or lesser extent; in times when marriages were harder to dissolve than they are now, it was seen as something to aim for, a way of relating well. When we first fall into a relationship, this and other models spring into action automatically. It is only by becoming conscious of what we do that we can open up the possibility of doing something else.

This is not to say, of course, that the old rules for marriage are complete rubbish!

Along with some dead wood, there is a great deal that is healthy and vigorous. Allowing each other to have separate lives, realising that you can't stay on the heights all the time, learning to let go of hurts and move on – all these are old-fashioned virtues, and they are pure gold. The key is to become conscious of what really works for you, what brings your relationship alive and what deadens it. Until you become conscious of what you are doing, your relationships will tend to operate on several levels at once, with different – and often conflicting – models operating in different areas. You will chart an erratic course between your own projections and expectations; between what you were taught and what you have learned, and between comfortable habits and the urge to expand. Occasionally, you will catch glimpses of your partner.

At the other end of the spectrum of possibilities is the longing that seemed to be fulfilled by falling in love in the first place – the longing to find true partnership, true meeting, an intimacy that leaves no room for compromise. Is such a thing possible? I believe that it is, and I also believe that falling in love offers you a glimpse of what may be. It is the ultimate con-trick, part of the divine plan to lure you into relationship. How else would you ever be persuaded, in cold blood and in your right mind, to let down your defences for long enough to engage with anyone else on such an intimate level?

But if it really is a con-trick, it is also much more than that. On the spiritual level, the ecstatic experience of being in love feeds you and brings you alive. On the level of the psyche and the emotions, it offers you an incomparable opportunity to wake up to yourself. And on the down-to-earth level, it gets you into relationship. You can't stay in love at the same intensity, but if you follow the ground rules we've talked about and keep open the space for intimacy, you will find that this paves the way for something deeper, truer and, in the end, much more satisfying.

Divine madness

All of this may sound like a complete dismissal of romance as a worthwhile way of engaging with other people. It isn't. As something of a love addict myself, it has been part of my journey to look long and hard at what was actually going on for me, and to penetrate beyond the unrealistic expectations I started out with. At the same time, I celebrate falling in love as one of the most wonderful and blissful experiences available to us. If it is madness, it is divine madness.

If we are not mindful, the way we structure our lives these days can result in the dangerous forces of passion and free creativity getting squeezed out, denied any place in the plan. The price we pay for that is that they become far more dangerous, far more likely to erupt without warning and wreak havoc in our orderly existence. However, if instead we start from the premise that these forces are at the centre of our aliveness, and that the needs of the spirit are just as imperative as the body's needs for food and drink, then the whole picture is turned around. Falling in love can be seen as the fire of the spirit burning more brightly, and you can honour it as it deserves, without necessarily investing too much in the possibility of relationship with the beloved. In the best sense of the word, it is a self-centred experience.

When you truly recognise this, you gain the power of choice. It is up to you what you do with it. You might choose to enter into relationship, or you might choose to consider, as Paul did, what you can learn from being in love. It could be that there is a part of yourself that is seeking expression. It could be that you have not allowed enough space for spirit in your life, and that it is finding this way to break through. Beyond all the attempts to find meaning, you can simply choose to enjoy, to rejoice in this wonderful gift that has come to you.

Beyond the illusion

Falling in love, like any other manifestation of spirit in our lives, remains essentially a mystery. There is something that remains beyond our best attempts at analysis, and this is as it should be. The greatest truths can only be lived, not understood. What you can bring to it, what transforms it from an unconscious acting out that may or may not lead on to relationship and new growth, is your awareness and your commitment to truth.

Beyond all this is your willingness to be open to spirit, to let go of control and be swept away, to revel in the gift of ecstasy and communion with the divine. I don't think many people have ever regretted that part of being in love. It is the part that we truly long for. When you recognise this, you free yourself from the need to control what happens between yourself and the beloved, and you can open yourself more fully to your own aliveness.

Paradoxically, when you do that, you also open yourself to the possibility of aliveness in relationship. When both partners own their own potential, their own divinity, they are truly ready to love and honour another human being. That is where relationship really takes off; not in the romance at the start, but growing slowly through the patient work of unpicking and rebuilding. If you do your work well, the rewards can be beyond your dreams.

The next step

In this chapter we have looked at how being in love takes you into a place of ecstasy. This experience is its own reward. You may get into a relationship with the person you are in love with, but you will find that your projections will eventually wear thin. We have looked at how to call them home to yourself, and set your beloved free from your expectations and fantasies. In the next chapter we begin to explore what happens if you stay with the relationship.

Chapter 2
Soulmates or Cell Mates?

If, in your lifetime, you can love one other human being, you will have achieved a great deal.
Rainer Maria Rilke, German poet, 1875–1926

'I don't know why anyone bothers with relationships. I've been hurt so many times. It's much easier just to be on my own and look after myself.'

These words were spoken by a client of mine a few years ago. Jim was in his mid-thirties and had been alone for eight years. He seemed, at first, content with the life he had made for himself, but just below the surface detachment lay pain, a seething anger and frustration, and complete bewilderment with the way relationships had let him down again and again.

Why is it so hard?

Falling in love simply happens to you; it takes no effort. Staying in love, on the other hand, takes commitment, energy, insight and wisdom. But why are intimate relationships so difficult? What happens to the intense delight and the passion that you feel at the beginning of a new relationship, and how is it that this so often degenerates into chaos and bitterness, or a state of compromise that leaves both partners half alive? Is it wiser to give up on the whole enterprise, like Jim, and deal with your loneliness as best you can? If we tried and failed so many times with any other kind of project we set our minds to, from driving a car to learning to read and write, we would have given up long ago. Looked at rationally, it makes no sense.

Relating, however, does not have much to do with reason. The force that drives you to keep trying arises in the heart, not in the head. Its roots are in the rich, dark soil of your emotions, and its expression in your life is often inarticulate and raw – not open to understanding and analysis except through slow and careful work. I have supported many thousands of people as they struggle with this work and try to make some sense out of the emotional tangles they get into. In my own life, I struggle continually with the demands and challenges of intimate relationships. Out of all this has grown the understanding that we emerge from childhood, as a rule, very poorly equipped to engage with each other in a meaningful and emotionally nourishing way.

The art of relating well is something that we have to discover for ourselves. Intellectually we can appear mature and wise, but emotionally most of us never grow up – and if we do, maturity comes in our forties and fifties rather than at eighteen or twenty-one. We reach it, if we reach it at all, slowly, haphazardly, and with many mistakes.

Much of my work is focused around the exploration and development of this art. What is a good relationship? How can you get better at it? If your motivation for change comes from getting it wrong – as of course it usually does – then what does getting it right look like? Alongside the work of dealing with crisis, stagnation, loneliness and all the other ways in which relationships can come to grief comes the building of new and healthier ways of relating.

What is the point?

As you work to create good relationships with your lovers, children, friends, family and workmates, so you learn more about yourself. When the ways of relating that you were taught by your elders and betters – themselves adrift in a rapidly changing world – don't work any more, you have the chance to replace them with ways that do work, ways that reflect who you really are, rather than who somebody else thought you should be.

Your explorations into relationships with other people can open you up to parts of yourself that are dormant or stunted. The people to whom you relate, even superficially, hold up mirrors to you; mirrors in which, if you have sufficient courage, humility and the desire to grow, you may catch glimpses of who you really are. Perhaps you are constantly meeting people who are angry. What does that say about you? It may be that you are not expressing your own anger, so they are doing it for you, or perhaps you have something to learn about coping with other people's anger. Either way, there is an opportunity here to become more conscious of who you are.

As you become more conscious of who you are, and recognise what drives you to behave as you do and feel what you feel, so you begin to open up the possibility of change. You can move to a place where you are no longer at the mercy of events, of other people and of your own unconscious patterns. The range of choices available to you increases as you move to a position where you are not a victim, but a creator. Life in general becomes a lot more fun, as you no longer need to expend your vital energy on holding on to ways of being that do not serve you well.

Have you ever thought about how much vital energy it costs to hide your vulnerability, to suppress your anger, to keep up the nice guy facade? Don't you sometimes long just to be in integrity with whatever it is you are feeling in the moment? I can share that with my partner, Amanda, and I can promise you that it is worth all the heartache, all the hurt on both sides, to come through to a place where we can simply be human together.

That doesn't mean, of course, that we have stopped hurting ourselves and each other, or that our feelings and needs are always in harmony. What kind of inhuman relationship would that be? What it does mean is that we have changed, and are changing, some of the ways of behaving that didn't work for us. It means that we try to stay open to each other, to be with our feelings – whatever they are – and to listen for the messages that lie beneath the temporary outbursts of madness. We have developed structures that hold our relationship together, which remain standing when the storms have passed.

There is no such thing as a perfect relationship. There is no ideal partner waiting out there somewhere. There are only people, men and women. Some may be easier to relate to than others, but all of us are carrying baggage, and all of us could do with a helping hand from time to time. In order to be able to relate, we all have to learn how to make changes in ourselves and in the way we do things. So the first skill that we need to acquire – not just in relationships, but in all areas of our lives – is the understanding of what changing actually means, and how to go about it.

Three steps towards change

Before you can begin the work of replacing bad habits with good ones – to put it very simply – you have to go through the process of bringing them, as fully as you can, out of the shadows where they have their beginnings and into the light of day. As long as you remain unconscious of what drives you to behave as you do, you have no choice but to repeat the old patterns. It is not enough to say that next time will be different.

I had a client recently who came to me after his partner left him, because, as he admitted, 'I wasn't able to support her when she needed it.' Charles is a management executive in his early forties, and he had always been very clear that he wanted a strong woman. 'In the past, when I've glimpsed the needy side of my current partner, I've always run.' This had happened enough times now for him to recognise the pattern, and he truly wanted the next time to be different, but he did not yet understand what it was that he was doing, or not doing, to create his situation. We'll look more closely at Charles's story below.

Between the desire to change and the reality of doing it differently, there are three steps to take. They will appear again and again in this book, for whatever the problem may be, the same process must be followed on the way to transformation. The three steps involve noticing what you are doing, becoming aware of the choices that you have and forming an intention for the future. Let's look at them here in more detail.

1. NOTICING

Until you begin to notice how you go about things, you can't change them. 'How?' is a more useful question to ask than 'Why?' at this stage. Finding reasons for your behaviour is important, and we do have a deep need to find meaning in what we do, but understanding why we act in a particular way does not necessarily help to change it. Noticing means focusing on where things go wrong, and becoming aware of what exactly is going on for you at that point. The help of loving friends, or perhaps a counsellor or a therapist, is essential; you can't see your own blind spots.

If we look at the example of Charles, whom I mentioned above, the first step is to be specific. I asked him to recall, in detail, an incident in which his ex-partner Jane had asked – directly or indirectly – for support, and he had failed to give it. What happened between them? What did they say to each other, and how was he feeling at each point?

Then I suggested that he imagine that Jane was present, and tell her what was going on for him. He also switched roles, speaking for Jane as he imagined she would be feeling. What began to emerge was that Charles could not bear to acknowledge his own neediness. He was a self-made businessman, deeply imprinted with the conviction that to be needy or vulnerable was to be weak. He had got by until now by denying that he had a needy side at all, but the price he paid was that he could not handle need in his partners either. He had always felt compelled to end his relationships as soon as the issue arose, so they never really got off the ground – that is until Jane, whose armour was in some ways even stronger than his, turned the tables on him.

It hurt; and with the hurt came the beginning of change. Charles was forced to admit to himself that he was vulnerable and needy, and that vulnerability and strength are not mutually exclusive. In fact, vulnerability and true strength go hand in hand. He had mistaken armouring for strength – as we often do – and he began now to learn that only by knowing and honouring our own vulnerability can we become truly strong. At the same time, he began to understand that if he had a needy side, then so would his partner. It seemed to me that the next time could indeed be different.

Out of this kind of close focusing, insights arise. When someone is in distress it is hard for them to see clearly. Pain casts a blanket of fog, obscuring the shape and perspective of things; and when you are in pain you tend to try to find ways of avoiding it, which takes you further away from awareness. But if, instead, you stay with it, the picture begins to change. A landscape begins to emerge, and there will be landmarks that you recognise, signs that you've been this way before. Noticing, and doing whatever you need to do to honour the feelings that you uncover, allows you to trace paths through the wilderness, and begin to make sense of your life. Once you know what it is that you feel and what it is that you do, you gain the power to choose.

2. MAKING CHOICES

There are always more choices than you think there are. As children, we model ourselves on the adults around us. We can't help doing this, but in the process we shut out an infinite number of other possible ways of being. We become imprinted with just a few tried and tested ways of acting and reacting. Then, when we encounter a new situation, when we attempt intimacy with someone whose conditioning may be very different, we get stuck.

I have often worked with couples who have run into an impasse like this, where the only option left seems to be to separate and so step out of the situation altogether, even though there may still be love between them.

A good example is that of Bill and Sarah, who had been living together for three years when I met them. Sarah wanted to leave Bill because, although they still cared deeply for each other, she had come to feel stifled and powerless in the relationship. Caught by her wish not to hurt him by leaving, she had slid into depression, and was unable to see a way out that would suit them both.

Eventually, Sarah decided that for her own sake, she had to leave. With that decision, she regained her aliveness and her power, and as the depression lifted, all sorts of new perspectives began to open up. She had never lived alone before, and had not even considered the possibility, but now she saw that she could leave and still stay in the relationship. More than that, it allowed the relationship to grow, so that Bill, as well as Sarah, found that his needs were met more fully.

You can't change the other person in the partnership. Nor does it help to lay blame on either side. What you can do is to become aware of what drives you (Step 1), and then consider your options. Awareness opens up your vision and allows you to gain a wider perspective. From a higher vantage point, all sorts of new possibilities can be seen. Moreover as in the first step, other people – especially the partner with whom the problem has arisen – can help you to open up to these possibilities.

The next step is therefore to consider your options and to allow yourself the space to be creative, even to play a little. Doing things differently feels strange and it takes time to get used to new paths. Trying it out in less emotionally loaded areas can help. If you are normally careful with money, for instance, you could allow yourself some outrageous extravagance; or if money slips through your fingers, allow yourself to notice where it goes, and keep an exact account for a month or so. How does it feel to break the rules? Sidestep the usual routine; practise lateral thinking. Flexibility in one area, if you bring awareness to it, has a way of spreading into other areas as well.

3. FORMING INTENTIONS

Once you have noticed what you do or what you feel and thus freed yourself to look at the choices available to you, you are ready to take the next step in full awareness and taking full responsibility for yourself. This means formulating your intentions as clearly as you can, and committing yourself to bringing them into reality.

Again, it helps to be specific. 'I intend to become a better human being' is not much use to anyone. Changing happens little by little, with occasional dramatic breakthroughs, and it is on the level of the particular, the small scale, that you can attain it. Also, positive intentions are better than negative ones: 'I will not lose my temper with the children' is far less useful than 'I will play a game with the children for half an hour on three evenings a week', for example – and even that may be asking too much. The commitments you make must be achievable, otherwise you simply set yourself up to get it wrong again.

Here, too, friends can act as supporters and loving witnesses, reminding you of your intentions and encouraging you along the way. The idea is to make it as difficult as possible to slip back into the old habits, so any device you can think of to help you achieve this is worth a try.

Exercise 3
Steps towards change

STEP 1. DECIDE WHAT YOU WANT TO CHANGE

From the first exercise in Chapter 1, you should have quite a few suggestions for things to work on, given to you by your friends and your partner. Choose one that appeals to you – perhaps the one that made you feel most ashamed when you heard it! If you haven't done the exercise, take some time to consider what you'd like to change in yourself. What do you feel uncomfortable about? If it's something fairly vague, like 'I lose my temper too easily', break it down to a more specific level. Think of a particular trigger that gets you angry, and focus on that one hot-spot. The more specific you can be, the more likely you are to succeed – and whatever you do, don't set yourself up to fail at this game!

Now apply the three steps outlined above. Let's take the example I gave in Chapter 1 (*see page 5*): your friends get annoyed with you because you are always late to meet them.

STEP 2. NOTICE HOW YOU DO IT

The next time you are going out to meet one of your friends, try to stay conscious of what you are doing. Do you postpone getting ready so that there isn't enough time? Do you make one last phone call, read the paper or stop on the way for some shopping? Is the appointment with your friend the last thing on your list? Don't try to do it differently at this stage, just notice. When you do get there, if you've asked your friend to help you with the problem, talk about what you noticed. They may have some further insights to offer. If you want, you can talk about it with your partner as well, but be careful: you don't want them sitting in judgment on you. You need allies, not critics.

STEP 3. MAKE YOUR CHOICES

Now you have the chance to change the record. There might be some very small adjustments to make, like not sitting down to check your email just before you go out. Or you might need to do something more drastic – to sweep aside all the clutter that gets in your way. Make the meeting your top priority; imagine you were going to meet someone famous or important, someone who has a present to give you that you won't get if you're late. Someone who really matters to you . . .

How does that feel? If it really was someone that important, you wouldn't just be on time, you'd be early, wouldn't you? So maybe this friend isn't that special after all – in which case, why did you take the risk of asking them to give you honest feedback about yourself? You can't have it both ways. If your relationships didn't matter to you, you wouldn't be reading this book. And if they do matter, they deserve some respect.

So be early, not just on time. Take something to do in case you have to wait for your friend. A new habit takes around thirty days to wear itself a groove; after that, it doesn't need effort any more. And the appreciation you'll get from your friends will do a lot to help the process along.

One client of mine, a young man who was studying computer programming, was near to breaking point when he came to see me. He lived with his wife and children in a small house, and the room in which he worked was next to the room where the children played. The noise they made, just by doing what children do, made it impossible for him to concentrate, and he was constantly losing his temper with them. His rage frightened him, and so did the realisation that he was in danger of losing his family altogether.

There was not enough space in the house to move further away. Somehow, the needs of everyone had to be met in a way that did not lead to conflict. After much discussion with me and with his partner, he decided to change tack completely. Instead of trying to avoid the children and shaming them in their play, he resolved to play with them between 6 and 6.30 every evening. His partner would then give them their supper – a little later than usual – and put them to bed, which gave him two hours or so of uninterrupted study. It also created the space to give the children some positive attention; and once they were party to the plan, they helped to make sure that his new intentions were carried out.

There will be plenty of examples of these three steps in later chapters, as you look at how change can come about in various aspects of your life. Alongside this, the 'How?' part of making changes, comes the need to become conscious of the qualities you must develop to sustain good relationships. It doesn't just happen automatically, but you have to get hurt a few times before you can begin to appreciate this. The point at which you start to ask yourself questions like, 'Where did I go wrong?', 'What happened to the magic between us' or 'How could he/she do this to me?', is the point at which you have the chance to examine and improve your relationship skills.

At the heart of the book is the concept that there is a set of key skills that are needed to make relationships work. Some you learn from your parents and peers, but along with the useful conditioning that you may gain in childhood comes a great deal that either gets in the way or is actively destructive to mature relationships. It is one of the challenges of adulthood to sort through this mixed legacy, consciously adopting what is good as your own, setting aside whatever does not serve you well and finding new ways of relating that work better.

From past to present

There is an urgency about this work that is unique to our times. In the West, the world has changed almost beyond recognition within the lifetimes of our parents and grandparents. The structures they grew up with have fallen away. The expectations and guidelines that they – consciously and unconsciously – handed on to us do not match up to our reality, and we have to find new ones for ourselves.

Consider just a few of the major changes in the last hundred years. We can expect to live much longer and in better health than ever before, so that our growing time has been extended. In terms of intimate relationships, marriage for life might once have meant thirty or forty years at most; now, it could mean sixty or more. Where are the role models for this kind of relationship? In any case, although people do still get married, more than a third of marriages end in divorce or separation – and of those that don't actually break up, a large proportion are less than nourishing to both partners. People no longer expect to stay together for better or for worse. Divorce is easier than it used to be, and it no longer carries the strong social and religious stigma that it once did.

Likewise, the shame that used to darken the lives of children born to unmarried mothers has been left behind, and their rights in law are the same as those of legitimate offspring. Because state support is now available, women can – and increasingly do – bring up their children alone, and they can choose to leave unhappy or abusive relationships from which there was formerly no escape. Women's legal rights changed enormously in the twentieth century – women now have the right to vote, the right to retain their own property within marriage and the right to accuse their husbands of rape. The availability of reliable contraception for the last forty years has meant that, for the first time, women can control their own fertility.

All of these factors – many of which we now take for granted – have had the effect of dissolving much of the glue that used to hold relationships together. So what do we have left?

According to the models we have inherited, the proper place for intimate relationships is marriage, or at least lifelong partnerships. Marriage used to provide for the disposition of property, the rearing of children in a shared household and a clear division of labour – the man, typically, worked to earn money, and the woman looked after the home and the children. It was expected that the married couple would have exclusive rights in each other's sexuality – at least overtly – and that they would look to each other for companionship and emotional intimacy.

Nowadays, however, it is actually quite uncommon to find all of these factors held within the framework of a marriage or partnership, although some of them may be. More people live alone or with new partners, and children may live with one parent or the other. Women are no longer expected to stay at home with children unless they choose to do so.

Choice is the key, in many ways. Your parents, and grandparents even more so, did not have, or did not allow themselves, this freedom to choose. Marriage was for life. What this meant, in terms of the quality of their relationships, was the understanding that since the external forms of partnership must be preserved, its emotional and spiritual sides had to come second.

Freda is a client in her seventies, who now lives in a nursing home. She is bright, aware and intelligent. Her husband Eric died six years ago, and her story is that her marriage was a long and happy one. Some time ago, during one of our sessions together, she talked of waking up feeling very sad and tearful, but being unable to cry. When I asked what stopped her, she recoiled a little, and then said, 'I haven't been able to cry since I was a child. When I was with Eric and I felt tearful, he used to pat me gently on the shoulder, and say, "Please don't do that, dear."'

Other factors that emerged in the course of our therapy time made it clear that this was indeed a happy relationship, because both parties accepted without question that the husband was the lord and master. If one partner always calls the shots and the other agrees to that, of course there will be no conflict – and absence of overt conflict is one of the traditional ways to judge the success of a relationship. Without conflict, it is unlikely that there will be much room to grow, but personal growth did not come very high on the traditional agenda.

Emotional well-being, in fact, was something of a hit-and-miss affair, and the guidelines for emotional behaviour, then as now, were passed on by example – whatever your elders *said* you should do, what they actually taught you was to do as they did. You learn by absorption, long before you are old enough to understand and give meaning to what you learn, and it is these lessons that stick deepest.

What you learn from your elders, what worked for them within the limits that were set, amounts to the practice of the art of compromise. Arguments and the expression of anger in general were unpleasant, and to be avoided if at all possible. Therefore, areas of conflict were simply not dealt with, or one partner gave way, swallowed their feelings and had to deal with them in various indirect ways. A couple learns by trial and error what flows easily between them, and what is dangerous ground. If conflict is to be avoided, the dangerous ground must be fenced off, and you must venture only where it is safe to go.

The cost of compromise

The trouble is that swallowed feelings do not simply disappear; however hard you try to deny them, reason them out of existence or find some safe way of dealing with them, they have a habit of leaking out somehow. The safest course is to turn them inwards onto yourself, where they manifest as physical or emotional illness, or loss of energy.

My client, Linda, is a typical example of what can happen when you try to compromise. She is twenty-nine years old, and she got married at nineteen in order to escape from what she described as a sterile home life. She first came to see me after having been treated with Prozac (an anti-depressant drug) for a few months. When she returned to the doctor for a fresh prescription, he wisely refused to give her more of the drug and sent her to me instead.

She appeared strikingly attractive, energetic and open – in fact, not at all depressed. What really struck me was that she was immobilised by the conflict within her. 'Colin is a really nice man – good with the children, kind and generous. When I married him, he was twenty-one years old and already middle-aged. I didn't know any better then, and I was happy for the first eight years. We have three lovely children, a nice car and enough money to live on. I feel so ungrateful, but this relationship is smothering me. I enjoy going out, being with people and having fun. Colin just wants to put his feet up at the end of the day, and although he never says it in so many words, I constantly sense his disapproval of me. He does say I've changed, and not necessarily for the better.'

Linda's depression arose, as it so often does, because she perceived her situation as hopeless. In her relationship with Colin there was no room for expansion, no space for aliveness and excitement and passion. Like so many of us, Colin seemed to have buried his own need for these things so deeply that he was not even aware of his loss, and Linda's increasing desperation could only confuse and threaten him.

Linda herself began by saying that she was confused, but as I listened to her it became obvious that she was not confused at all. In her heart, she knew exactly what was going on. This confusion arises when there is conflict about what is real. Linda's upbringing had led her to believe that her life contained all the ingredients for happiness. Her husband, her family – and to start with, her doctor as well – supported this view, which meant that there must be something wrong with her. There was no one in her life to whom she could talk without being judged in some way, until she was sent to me.

My task was simply to listen, to help her sift through the layers of pain and guilt and desperation and hopelessness, until her own wisdom, the wisdom that none of her family wanted to hear, could emerge. Here, there was no confusion. Linda knew that unless she could find nourishment for her spirit within her marriage, it would simply starve. She would become truly depressed, and dependent on tranquillisers to deaden her pain and help her bear the burden of her life.

We explored the possibility of change within the marriage. What was Colin prepared to do to keep it alive? The answer was, not enough. He continued to deny that there was anything wrong, and he could not understand what Linda was trying to say to him. For a relationship to grow, there must be willingness on both sides. Linda was faced with an agonising choice: to stay, and try to cut herself down to size, or to end the marriage. In fact, as I sensed quite early on, she had made her choice some time ago. All she needed was the permission to know her own heart, and the courage to act on that knowledge.

Eventually, after a couple of short separations and much heartache on all sides, she left. It took her a year to come to peace with her decision and begin to find a direction for herself, but in her own words, 'The decision was the best choice I've ever made.' Linda's predicament is typical of the kind of struggle facing women in our times, as they realise that they don't have to sell their souls any longer in order to fit into a restrictive and suffocating mould.

Doctors' lists are full of women on tranquillisers or other medications, trying to deal with symptoms like these. Besides taking tranquillisers or becoming physically ill, there are plenty of other indirect ways of handling emotional pain or lack of fulfilment. Some of them work better than others. Pouring all your energy into work is an obvious example. Others are less acceptable or less easy to justify, although no less common: drinking, food abuse, becoming depressed, having affairs. The cost of avoiding emotional engagement is higher for some of us than for others, but there is one price that we all have to pay, and that is in terms of aliveness. Each time we draw back from potential conflict, each time we choose silence or conciliation rather than expressing what is true for us, we shut down; we die a little.

So why bother?

And yet, here is the central paradox. Why do we enter into a relationship in the first place? *Because it is one of the main places in which we find our aliveness.* We are social creatures; we exist in a web of relatedness to ourselves, to the people around us, to other sentient beings, to the world we live in and to the divine, whatever our concept of that may be.

We can't live without relationships, and within them, we crave intimacy. We find our greatest aliveness, we feel most fulfilled, where we engage most closely with others – when we are in love, make love or create something with another person: a child, a piece of work, a shared experience. We find it, in fact, when we venture onto the dangerous ground where conflict may arise.

37

So, what we have left is a challenge that is unprecedented in our history, one for which we have no role models and no paths to follow. The old structures that used to enmesh our intimate relationships are not as binding as they used to be. We can never return to the world of our parents, even if we regret the passing of some of its qualities. We are free to enter into relationship for its own sake, if we choose to do so – and most of us do make that choice.

I know plenty of people who are not in intimate relationships right now, but very few of them want to stay that way for the rest of their lives. We need intimacy, and our need is constantly at odds with our fear of being hurt or let down, our trust betrayed. The old models are no help to us; in fact, they are worse than useless to our attempts to relate honestly, for they do not match the way that we actually are. It is up to us to develop new relationship skills for the new territory that we are entering. In the next chapter we begin to look at these skills.

In summary

In this chapter, we've looked at some of the reasons why we get into relationships, and why it is worth learning to get better at them. How do you start to make changes? There are three steps towards change: noticing what you do, making choices and forming new intentions.

Chapter 3
Where the Work Begins

After the ecstasy, the laundry.

Zen saying

In an ideal world, perhaps, you would acquire the right skills before entering into a relationship – rather like training for a career. In real life, however, you have no choice but to pick up the training as you go along, trying to build strong foundations for a house in which you're already living. If you don't choose to do this it will collapse, and you will be left either with no relationship, or with the empty shell of one.

What are these strong foundations? In this chapter we take a look at some of the most basic relationship skills, and how you can learn to use them. There's no excuse – we are all capable of learning new skills. We can come to recognise what works for us, and what actually gets in the way of intimacy. Not all of what you learned in childhood has to be thrown away, and some of it could turn out to be pure gold in relationship terms. You don't really know how you'll handle a situation until you're in the middle of it. Besides, the skills that you need are not truly new; 'underdeveloped', perhaps, is a better way of describing them.

These key skills, or building blocks of good relationships, have emerged from my work over the years, as I see the same issues coming up for clients again and again. Some are very simple and relatively easy to learn or to improve upon. Others are more difficult, requiring a greater degree of self-knowledge and emotional maturity.

Key skills in relationships

The first two skills are about the ability to listen and the ability to appreciate. At one level they are very straightforward, but once you learn how to practise them in the obvious ways, other avenues for communication begin to open up that can have profound and dramatic effects on the quality of your relationships.

The third basic skill concerns the building and maintaining of a strong support structure. It has less to do with the way you behave within a relationship, and more to do with the setting in which it is placed. For the creation of a dynamic, flexible and evolving partnership, support is vital.

THE ART OF LISTENING

In a conversation between two people, what usually happens is that while one is talking, the other is filtering what he or she hears, interpreting, making judgments and getting ready to reply as soon as the first person stops. Effectively, we take it in turns to talk about our own experiences or observations.

In a discussion about something 'out there' – an exchange of ideas and information – this works fairly well. If the subject is feelings, however, it won't even take you to first base. When you are trying to express your feelings – and this is an art in itself, of which more later – you need to be heard without judgment, without interpretation, and without your experience immediately being capped by that of the other person. This matters most of all when the other person is a partner, a lover or someone equally close to you. To put it very simply, you need to be *received*.

This need to be received, to be heard, is a very basic one, and it is one of the things that moves you to seek relationships in the first place. You know when you have been truly received, when someone has really listened or 'been there' for you; you grow quiet inside, your hunger is satisfied. If you are not heard, you remain restless, unappeased.

Tom and Debbie were stuck in a vicious circle. He felt that she didn't love him enough. She found his need overpowering, and put up defences against it. Ten years on, they had reached stalemate; they hardly ever made love, and avoided spending time together. They were miserable, but neither could hear what the other had to say without springing to their own defence.

In therapy, with myself to hold the space, they started to do what they could not do alone; they began to listen to each other. Freed from the need to respond to Tom's complaints, Debbie could acknowledge the insecurity that drove him to seek constant reassurance. In turn, he could see that she was repelled by his needy behaviour, but that she did truly love him. In being seen – at last! – they both began to feel safer. Gradually, they were able to start exploring new ways of relating that satisfied both of them.

Young children demonstrate this very clearly before they learn ways to hide or suppress what they feel. When you ignore them, give them partial attention or try to reason or shame them out of their feelings, they simply try harder. As soon as they feel heard, it is finished, and on to the next thing. Children are good people with whom to practise the art of listening.

What stops us from listening to each other? Essentially, it comes down to fear. There is fear that you will not be heard yourself, that if one partner is heard then the other can't be (this is a very common dynamic in couple relationships). There is also fear that the feelings of the other person will hurt or damage you in some way, so that you must put up your defences before they even begin to speak.

Underneath it all, there is fear of the very thing that you long for, namely true meeting, open and vulnerable and unguarded. What might happen then? In that place of true meeting, you risk being truly naked with each other – and in your nakedness you are defenceless, able to be deeply wounded or almost destroyed. How can you ever dare to take such a risk? Actually, you have no choice, if you really want a healthy, dynamic relationship. You can put off making the choice for a thousand seemingly valid reasons; you can go on marking time until the end of your days. But why waste this precious gift of life and passion? You can go beyond safety into love – and, paradoxically, that is where true safety lies. It is the one true shelter from the storm, right at the heart of it.

The only way that I know of to develop the art of listening is to do it. Like a lot of skills, it improves with practice. Try the exercise below; if you've done the earlier exercises, you won't find it too strange. Make it short and light at first; use your five minutes to talk about your day, the things you've seen and done. If it feels too scary to try it with your partner, do it first with a friend. And if you have children who are old enough, you can do this all together, using a speaking object (and making sure an adult is keeping time!). It is never too soon to start learning how to listen.

Exercise 4
Learning to listen

Begin, as usual, by choosing a time and place that won't involve any interruptions, and make sure you are not in a hurry. When you have decided who will go first, take a minute to sit in silence, and bring your full attention to the present moment. Then, while one of you speaks for five minutes, the other listens, not interrupting or commenting or giving any feedback; just listening with the best attention they can muster. Listening is not passive – it is both active and receptive. For the listener, it is an exercise in learning simply to be present.

When it's your turn to speak, be sure that you talk only about yourself. Make statements beginning with 'I feel' or 'I think'. Don't be drawn into talking about other people, especially the one sitting in front of you. This is your space, and yours alone.

Notice how difficult this can be. You may feel your partner never really listens to you, but getting what you want can be scary, too. Notice if you waste your time, fidget, create distractions or ramble on about nothing rather than taking the opportunity to take centre stage. Then next time, you can choose to do it differently.

Make an agreement to do this exercise, if possible, at least three or four days of the week. After all, it will only take about fifteen minutes each time – you can't possibly argue that you don't have the time! Keep it up for four weeks; after that, you should find that a new and positive habit has been formed. It becomes one of the rhythms of your relationship. After this time, you may not need to do it quite so often; you will find the level that works best for you. In between, don't analyse it together; if you want to talk about what you're finding out, use a trustworthy friend (with your partner's permission). But work on it yourself, using the three steps outlined in Chapter 2 (*see pages 25–29*): notice what you do, choose what you want to change and how, and focus your intentions on small and achievable things.

In the day-to-day flow of life, of course, we never stop to listen to each other in a structured way like this, but there are plenty of other ways in which to practise the art. Part of the process of building a relationship, for instance, involves learning the language of the other. The same words can carry a very different meaning depending upon how they are spoken, and by whom.

LEARNING EACH OTHER'S LANGUAGE
Relationships can all too easily come to grief because the two people involved simply do not understand each other's language. I have worked with too many couples who are locked in bitter conflict, each desperately trying to make the other hear, and each completely missing, or misinterpreting, what is being said by the other.

A good example is that of Nick and Judith, with whom I worked over a period of three years or so. At the start of this time, Nick had just left Judith and their three children in a state of acute crisis. The next stage was a long separation, during which they could hardly talk to each other outside their therapy sessions. By the end of the three years, they could once again live together and take their partnership forward into uncharted territory. They were in their mid-thirties when I met them, both intelligent, articulate and intensely miserable together.

Nick was a quick-tempered man, like his father. His response when things did not work out as he wanted them, or when he felt hurt or under pressure, was to fly into a rage. He was never physically violent to Judith or the children, but he would shout, bang doors and sometimes storm out of the house. Beneath the rage, as he came slowly to understand, was a terror of being abandoned, of losing everything. He associated this with a time in early childhood when he was seriously ill, and according to the practice of the time, was taken away from his family and placed in isolation in hospital for several weeks. On a more everyday level, he also felt that his mother had not 'been there' for him emotionally.

Judith, on the other hand, was unable to see any of this. She found his anger terrifying. Her response was to freeze, to retreat inside herself where she could not be reached. She could not say what it was that she feared, but as we worked together, it began to emerge that her own father had beaten his children when they annoyed him. The survival strategy that she had adopted as a child had been to disappear as completely as she could.

Quite unconsciously, she was still doing this. At the merest hint of a threat she would shut down, becoming totally emotionally unavailable. This, of course, would incite Nick to further rage, and so a dreadful vicious circle had developed. Neither of them, as so often happens, could talk about it to their friends, who saw them as having a very good marriage, and were shocked when it suddenly fell apart.

On the surface, it appeared that Nick was the aggressor and Judith the victim. At a deeper level, however, they were not really interacting at all. Instead, each was coming from a position of hurt, and each was using the defence tactic that he or she had learned long ago. Nick's defence was rage, and Judith's was withdrawal. Both tactics have a dual purpose, in that they hide the users' real feelings, not only from others, but from themselves as well. So these two people, who so desperately needed to be heard, had found a very neat way to perpetuate the patterns of childhood. As Judith herself said, 'We got married because our neuroses were compatible.'

For Nick and Judith, the deadlock only ended when his leaving propelled them into therapy. In their sessions together, because a third person was present to hold the space for them and to act as both witness and interpreter, they began in time to get beyond the opening words of their familiar emotional dialogue. They began, in fact, to understand each other's language.

Once they learned to listen for the underlying messages, those messages began to be clearer, the defences less automatic. Judith came to know that, although she still felt afraid of Nick's anger, she had the power of choice over how to deal with it. If she withdrew when he became angry, as she had always done, nothing would change. But if she stood her ground and did not disappear, something different would emerge.

As Judith found her way to her own feelings of anger, they began to have real arguments. The child in her felt that to stand her ground was to invite some unspeakable retribution. Instead, as Nick felt himself to be met and heard, not only in his rage but in what lay beneath, his desperation began to subside. As he could see and hear Judith more clearly, it became less possible to react to her as he had learned to react to his mother. They could meet, sometimes, as adults. As adults, they could reveal their own pain and vulnerability, and offer each other support. Out of the wreckage of their marriage, a mature relationship began to grow.

So, listening can lead to some dramatic changes. When you listen skilfully you begin to notice. From the simple, everyday level of noticing when your partner is upset or tired or wanting to celebrate, it opens the door to deeper levels, and gives permission for the unheard parts of yourself to find expression. Noticing is the first step in becoming conscious. Once we are conscious of our patterns of behaviour, we have the opportunity to change them.

Listen quietly and with an open heart, and what you hear may not be what you expect. What have you got to lose?

Exercise 5
Decoding your partner's language

During the five-minute sessions together that you began in Exercise 4, use your listening time to notice how your partner communicates (or doesn't). Because there is no pressure on you to respond to what he or she is saying, you can give your full attention to what you see. For instance, how does he express hurt? Does he avoid it, go cold and distant, get angry or show it directly? When she is feeling guilty about something, does she justify herself, throw blame around or go into self-pity, or does she own her bad feelings? And so on; you will soon compile your own list!

You will begin to learn that some behaviours are a mask for other, more difficult feelings. The cues you picked up with your family, or with previous partners, may not work at all in this situation, as we saw in Nick and Judith's story. Noticing, once again, is the first step towards change. Once you understand what is really going on, your own responses will change. Understanding brings compassion. Where in the past you might have felt under attack, seeing through your partner's surface behaviour to the place where they are hurting allows you to step out of the cycle of conflict and respond directly to their vulnerability. The next time you run into this area of difficulty in your relationship, the old pattern of behaviour will have been loosened a little; you will have the choice to react differently. This, in turn, will give your partner permission to express what they are really feeling, rather than masking their emotions.

THE ART OF APPRECIATION

This, again, on the mundane level is laughably simple, but seriously under-practised. It means noticing when something about your partner – or anyone else, for that matter – pleases you, and saying so. How often do you notice that they are looking good, have taken time and trouble over some household task or have been there for you in some way? When you do notice, how do you acknowledge it?

It is all too easy to take each other for granted, as you once took your parents for granted. Letting each other know that you are valued and appreciated is fundamental to the success of a relationship, and so often you simply forget or do not bother to do it. This doesn't mean being artificial or finding things to praise all the time. Rather, it means expanding and giving attention to the part of you that does value and appreciate.

Once again, there is much more to this than appears on the surface. What happens when someone pays you a compliment? We have plenty of ways to discount compliments, of course, but even if we do that, we are warmed a little. Our self-esteem gets a boost. Everyone likes to be appreciated; very few of us could not use a little more admiration. It draws you out, and you allow yourself to expand and be more expressive. And when people express themselves more, not to impress others or to take power in some way, but from a place where they feel truly good about themselves, they become more beautiful.

You learn from an early age to take on board what people say about you. If you receive praise for your efforts, admiration for your beauty and encouragement to explore your potential – as is the right of every child – you will believe that you are a praise-worthy and admirable person with much to offer in relation-ships, work and creativity. Your self-esteem will be high, and your life will be full and rich. Most of us do not receive such wholehearted affirmation, and we have places where we do not feel lovable or admirable in any way. We need help from our partners and those around us to be able to be in touch with our own beauty.

Mandy was an intelligent and lively girl in her twenties, but she felt that because she was not classically attractive, no man would ever love her. When she got together with Phil, it was clear to everyone who knew them that he did genuinely adore her. At their wedding reception, he made a lovely speech in which he praised her beauty, among many other compliments. Her response was to giggle and look away; she could not receive his appreciation.

Over the next few years, Phil tried in his straightforward way to heal Mandy's lack of love for herself by loading her with compliments at every opportunity. Every time, she would turn them aside, sometimes with acid and hurtful comments. Eventually, feeling hurt and rejected, he stopped trying. By the time they came to see me, the relationship was breaking down; he felt unable to express himself, and she felt increasingly unloved. It was as though she had to prove herself to be unlovable by driving him away, although love was what she desperately craved. Slowly, by doing structured work on listening and on appreciation, she was able to begin to believe that he did truly find her beautiful. He, in turn, could see that his love was being received, and got some long-overdue appreciation in his turn.

I say more about self-esteem in the next chapter, for it is the cornerstone of a good relationship. The point I want to make here is that appreciation is self-fulfilling. If you treat your partner like dirt, then that is what you will have to live with. If, on the other hand, you treat your partner like a goddess or a god, for even a tiny fraction of the time you spend together, you will be making space for something wonderful to emerge.

Exercise 6
Appreciation

Set up your time and place as before. This time, however, you are going to use your turn to speak to give your partner some appreciation. Tell them what you love about them, what you find admirable. Talk about the way they look, how they dress, how they go about their lives. Make sure that you say only positive things – don't lie, of course, but don't get into criticism. Take a couple of minutes each for this exercise.

When it's your turn to listen, try to stay open to what you are hearing. Some of it may surprise you! Notice how you can discount praise, turn it aside or reason it away. Notice if you are hoping for particular words from your partner, or expecting them not to appreciate you enough, or tell lies. These are also ways of not receiving what is actually being given to you, right now.

At the end, thank each other, but don't get into discussion about what was said or not said. For once, just let yourselves bask in mutual admiration.

Creating support

No one person can meet all our needs, yet so often you try to load all your demands on to one person, a partner who must be your sexual, emotional and spiritual companion to the exclusion of all others. Then, when you run into trouble with the relationship – as you almost certainly will – who else is there to talk to? And what happens when you're not part of a couple at all?

James was in his early forties. For the last three or four years he had been sure that he wanted to be a father, and now he felt that soon it would be too late. He was in relationship with a woman whom he liked and respected, but did not love in the way he felt was right for a relationship that would lead to having children and staying together for many years. There were too many ways in which they did not meet; she was not interested in intellectual discussion and the arts, did not play any sport and didn't enjoy going out with groups of their friends, as he did.

Crisis came; his partner became pregnant. James was very clear that he ought to stand by her and welcome this as a step forward. What he wanted to do, the work that he brought to therapy, was to *choose* to be with her wholeheartedly. The solution lay not in making the best of a bad job, but in creating a strong support structure so that the needs not met inside the relationship – for fun with friends, for physical activity and intellectual stimulation – would be met elsewhere, particularly with male friends. James had to let go of the idea that one woman could be everything to him, and accept that what they had was more than good enough.

Creating support is a skill that is fundamental to the building of a strong relationship, and yet one that is desperately undervalued and underdeveloped. You can't possibly hope to sustain a living, growing, intimate partnership with one other person unless you also have strong connections outside and around that partnership. Over-dependence on one exclusive relationship is fostered in our culture, with its horror of showing emotions in public and its exalted ideal of romantic love, but the plain truth is that nothing is more likely to bring about the death of true love that to overload it in this way.

Support can come from many sources, and the more of them you can draw upon, the better. Each has its strengths and its weaknesses, and sometimes one will be more appropriate than another. The main places where you look for support are your family and friends. Beyond those, there are support groups, some with a specific theme like Alcoholics Anonymous, and others like the groups I run, where people come to work on themselves and make new friends. When you want one-to-one help, there are professional counsellors or therapists. There are other resources, such as books or solitary meditation, which you can explore on your own, but in the end there is no substitute for warm human contact.

SUPPORT IN THE FAMILY

If you have maintained close ties with your parents or brothers and sisters, this may be the first place you go when you are in distress. Beware – even the wisest and most loving parents find it hard to allow their children to be in pain. It is hard for them to suspend judgment, not to blame, when they see you going through agonies with your chosen partner. They cannot help taking sides; and although that may be balm to your wounds at times, it may not always benefit the relationship. Their first concern is for your survival and well-being, not for the survival of your partnership. That means that it will be up to you to decide, step by step, whether their support is appropriate or not.

Janice was a successful businesswoman in her early thirties. All her friends saw her as someone who had her life completely sorted, but she had a guilty secret; in private, she would binge on chocolate. When her weight ballooned, she would go on a savage diet. The weight would fall away, then she would binge again. She hated herself, and her shame made her unable to tell any of her friends about her problem. The only person she confided in was her mother.

In the course of therapy, she became conscious of a pattern: after seeing her mother she would go straight for the chocolate. As we focused on what went on between them, it became clear that Janice's mother – who knew all her weaknesses – was actually undermining her daughter with critical remarks and the expectation of failure. In fact, as she finally realised, her mother's advice was poisoning her.

After a lot of hesitation, she plucked up the courage to confide in a friend. To her surprise, what she received was not scorn or rejection, but support. Her friend, in fact, expressed relief at seeing 'the real you behind the perfect mask'. Instead of losing face, she gained it. She began to feel better about herself, and the old toxic cycle of behaviour began to lose some of its power.

For the rest of us, whose parents are less than perfectly wise and loving, the pitfalls are far deeper. When you first encounter difficulties with a partner you run up against two barriers: your own immaturity, and the limitations of the role modelling you

51

got from your parents. In other words, if part of the trouble lies in what you learned from them, you can't look to them for help. You have to find new role models, and helpers with wider vision.

So, families are a resource to be used with caution and awareness. In order to find the kind of support that you will need on your journey into adult relationship, you must look further afield.

SUPPORT FROM FRIENDS

The obvious next source of help in times of trouble is your friends. These are people with whom you have chosen to develop a connection, usually because of some experience or interest in common.

However, the connections that you make in this way may not work for you when it comes to opening up, showing emotional distress and being vulnerable. There is such a conspiracy of coping in our culture, such pressure not to show that we are in trouble, that very often we have to come to the point of complete breakdown before we will let the 'brave face' slip. I have counselled so many people who, although they may be surrounded by friends with whom they share work or play, do not feel that there is anyone with whom they can share pain, or talk honestly about what is closest to their hearts. Very often, we do not even have the language in which to speak about these things, and this is yet another new skill to learn.

Anna is a client of mine who is in her late fifties; a warm, wise, passionate and outgoing woman who is surrounded by friends and acquaintances. She has weathered many storms in her life, and she struck me at first as someone who had built up a very well-developed support system and knew how to use it. Recently, however, her resources had been stretched to their limit. Her mother, who was very emotionally demanding, had become too frail to live on her own any longer and had gone to live in a home. Anna saw that instead of sustaining her, the home was killing her; she hated it so much that she wanted to die.

In her compassion, Anna had her house remodelled so that her mother could come to live there. All her friends told her that she was crazy, but she could not bear to let her mother suffer; however, their relationship was very intense and demanding for her, and having her mother in her home proved to be every bit as difficult as her friends had feared.

She thought that she had sufficient support from her partner, but here her words provided the giveaway: 'He's incredibly patient and understanding, but I just can't keep taking from him. It's not fair.'

When I asked whether there were other friends to whom she could talk, she answered at once, 'Oh yes, lots!' I pressed her to be more specific. Who, exactly, could she go to? This time the reply was more hesitant: 'Well, there are a few . . .'. What emerged was that Anna, with her open heart and ready compassion, tended to be the one to whom others came with their troubles, and this one-sidedness had become a habit. Fortunately, once she had realised this, she could also see that there were ways to redress the balance, and chose two friends with whom she could begin to discuss things.

When you do try to opt out of the conspiracy and find friends with whom it is possible just to be in integrity with your feelings, it very quickly becomes clear who will be willing to take this journey with you and who will not. We have all experienced how some friendships lose their vitality while others endure when we make changes or go through crises in our lives. In fact, a crisis is often the very thing that opens the door to deeper intimacy with a friend, and although you may dread the thought of admitting that your life seems to be falling apart, the response that you get may surprise you. Consider how you would feel if someone you cared for let down their defences and showed you their need for a good friend. Would you feel put upon, or honoured? In the same way, if you are honest with yourself, you will know which of your friends would be honoured to receive your confidence.

In order to build a strong and flexible support system, it is necessary to discriminate. Once again, it is a question of noticing what goes on when you are with your friend, and making a conscious decision whether to invest your energy in this friendship, or not. Ask yourself how this would serve you. Do you feel energised after spending time with this friend, or are you drained? Do you support each other in your growing, or do you have an investment in staying as you are? When you are in pain, do you have to hide it, or will you be lovingly received?

If you are to grow and flourish, you need to surround yourself with a community of like minds, one that will honour creative selfishness in its members, celebrate playfulness and self-expression and accept you for who you are. Friends who are committed to the journey of self-fulfilment will be learning, as you are, how to care for themselves, to feel their own feelings and to find the paths through the maze of intimacy. In my own life, my close friends provide me with communion of spirit and emotional nourishment. I trust them to give loving support when I need it, and to challenge me when I need that too. One of the side effects of improving your self-esteem is that you become unwilling to settle for anything less in your friends; and if old friends won't or can't welcome a relationship rooted in truth and fearless integrity, then maybe it's time to move on.

I have talked about friends in the plural. This is very important, for one friend is not enough. As a therapist, I often meet people who have no intimate friends at all, but just as often a client will say 'Oh, but I do have one friend I can really talk to.' One is better than none, but still it will not always meet your needs. What happens when your dearest friend is away, or immersed in troubles of her own?

Carol was a client of mine who recently came close to suicide when her friend suddenly broke off all contact. Carol was going through a long depression and had been phoning her friend several times a day. Quite simply, the good will ran out. If you put all your eggs in one basket, this risk becomes very real. And even when the load is not so great, there will be comfortable places in any one friendship, mutual blind spots, unspoken contracts, that limit its potential as a tool for expansion and experimentation with new ways. Friends, like intimate partners, can also come to support each other in not growing.

How can you go about creating a network of friends that will both support you in your partner relationships, and enable you to meet those needs that one partner alone cannot fulfil? It may happen of its own accord, but just as you can't expect the 'right' partner to appear magically in your life one day, so it is unlikely that good friends will simply manifest themselves without any effort on your part. Even if they do, the friendship won't continue to flourish and develop unless you feed it.

And yet, it is also unnecessary to go looking for them. The places where you'll find them are places where most of us need to go in the course of our journey. As part of your self-unfolding, you will explore in many directions. If your need at the moment is to develop your potential for painting or dancing, playing sport or learning a language, for example, the obvious thing to do is to find a class or a group that focuses on this theme. There you'll find other people who are engaged in the same process of discovering themselves, and who are just as much in need of support as you are. Together, you can travel much further and faster than you can manage on your own – and have some good times along the way.

THERAPEUTIC GROUPS

Groups aren't for everyone, but they can have a part to play. A therapy group provides a wonderful source of people committed to personal development, ready to act as witnesses, play roles, give support and challenge where you are holding back. I love the richness and fertility of the group environment, the space that it offers to try out new ways of being with people who have no stake in the old ways. It is a superb place to begin repatterning your relationships, to take risks and make mistakes and see what happens when you really allow yourself to be vulnerable.

A lot of what goes on in the groups that I run is not strictly therapy at all. Recently, I held an ongoing group that ran for six weeks, one evening a week. At the first session there was the usual mixture of people, all bringing different issues and life experiences, including one woman who had never done any sort of therapeutic work before, and who was understandably very nervous.

During the evening we each talked a little about what we hoped to get from the group, and then we danced. Later, we listened while another woman spoke about her conflicting feelings as she tried to support her husband through a serious and potentially fatal illness. It was clear that she was in great need of support herself, and afterwards she lay down, with soft music playing, and the rest of us gathered around to give what we could through the loving touch of our hands. She cried a little, and some of us cried with her.

Afterwards, the newcomer remarked in wonder, 'I didn't think therapy was like this!' It isn't. Much of the work of therapy is hard, painful, stripping away illusions and confronting old wounds and fears. It demands stamina, strength, resilience and the willingness to face unpleasant truths. And yet, what is therapy? For me it is also about opening our hearts to each other, crying and laughing together, witnessing each other's pain and finding that there is healing in the act of witnessing.

There is more. Therapy is also about being joyful, being expressive, being passionate, being silly. Within the group, there is the opportunity to try out some of these neglected skills, too. 'Shit-shovelling', as a client once described it, is an essential part of the work, but the work is also about turning shit into compost, a rich source of nourishment for the potential self that is beginning to unfold.

This work, as a rule, is a gradual process. A weekend group won't transform your life, and any that make claims to do so should be avoided. What it may do is to move you, sometimes profoundly, and great things may come of that; but be careful. To get the most from a short group, you should have a good support structure already in place – good friends, a therapist, co-counselling, for example – which will help you to integrate and build on any shifts that may happen. Real change means practising a new way of operating again and again until it becomes established. This doesn't happen overnight, or even in a few days – but it need not take years, either.

I find that longer-running groups work best of all, because the bonding that happens between the group members becomes a powerful support structure in itself, a new 'family' in the best sense of the word. During the lifetime of a year-long group, for instance, 'work' done during a group meeting can be taken into everyday life and practised, and the changes that are set in motion can be brought back to the group at the next session. As well as being a crucible for transformation, the group provides the holding for its members that enables them to ground their transformations in reality.

COUNSELLING AND THERAPY

One-to-one work is quite distinct from group therapy, and although they overlap a great deal, it can answer different needs and bring out different responses. As a therapist, I see my role as that of a kind of midwife of the psyche, bringing my presence and attention to my clients as they give birth to themselves anew.

The therapeutic relationship is different from all our other relationships. It is also unique in history, a tool devised to help us find our way through uncharted territory. A therapist is not a priest or healer, or a friend or relative, although the relation-ship that is created may take on qualities that we recognise from other contexts. What we ask of a therapist is that he or she hold no investment in the way we are, no judgments or preconcep-tions that will keep us from finding out what is true for us. During therapy time, for one hour a week or whatever the contract may be, we ask that this other person be present for us, giving us total attention and unconditional acceptance. To the extent that the therapist is able to be present in this way, healing can happen. So much of the pain that we carry comes from not being heard, not being seen, not being allowed to be who we are, that this in itself is profoundly transformative. It is so rare in everyday life to be truly present with another person for more than a few seconds at a time that many of us have to begin simply by learning what it feels like.

Most people come into therapy in a state of crisis. Life is not working; problems are insurmountable. You get into the same messes again and again, driving round and round the same roundabout, unable to find the exit. Simply admitting that you can't do it on your own, that you need a helping hand, is the start of the process. Once begun, it takes its own course; you can use therapy as pain relief, a place to discharge tensions so that you can carry on with your life, or you can use it as an entry into self-transformation, and take that as far as you choose.

At the core of the relationship, the soil in which growth can take place, is the quality of attention that the therapist brings. You will know whether he or she is truly there for you by whether you feel safe to explore the deeper and darker levels of yourself, the places you are too frightened to go into on your own. If the therapist is denying something in you, or judging it as unwholesome or ugly in some way, the process cannot continue to unfold. I repeat, you will know. If you feel blocked, check out what is happening for your therapist; and if he or she is not open to being challenged, it may be time to move on. We are in the business here of repatterning, of building healthy and honest relationships, and in this one relationship, if nowhere else, you owe it to yourself not to settle for less.

The therapist's ability to accompany you on your journey springs from his or her own self-development and self-acceptance. I cannot be with a client in places I am not willing to go into for myself. I cannot be present with compassion, without judgment, unless I remember my own humanity. I cannot allow my client to reclaim his or her power, to rejoice as the magic and wonder of being alive are restored, if I am not comfortable with my own power, my own magic. And unless, at the end of the day, I can acknowledge the client as an equal, the therapeutic relationship will stop short of maturity.

The next step: caring for yourself

In this chapter, we have begun to look at some of the basic building blocks of relationships. To relate well, you need to be able to listen and to understand the other person's language, and you need to give them appreciation. We've also looked at the various kinds of support structures that we need if we are to succeed in our building. As we go on to consider further relationship skills, it is time to turn inwards and focus on one particular skill. Without this, your attempts at relating to others will be seriously handicapped from the outset. Before you can seriously begin the work of loving another, you have to learn to love yourself.

Chapter 4
Self-esteem – Learning To Love Yourself

The love for my own self is inseparably connected with the love for any other human being.

Erich Fromm, German writer, 1900–1980

Good self-esteem is the rock upon which relationships are built. All the work that I have done with people over the years leads back to this: my capacity to love another – not need, but truly love – is only as great as my capacity to love myself. If, therefore, I want to learn to relate with passion and aliveness and without fear, I must begin to put my own house in order.

What does it mean to love yourself? How do you lose your self-esteem, and how do you go about rebuilding it?

The loss of self-love

We are born beautiful. How do you judge that something or someone is beautiful? By your own response to it, the wonder or the pleasure or the heart-catching tenderness that it evokes in you. Babies and children evoke that response in all of us not too deadened by our own pain to feel it; it is their birthright.

Their beauty lies not only in their physical appearance, but also in their joy and vitality, the way they express themselves without self-consciousness, their vulnerability. We love these qualities in adults too, when we catch the occasional glimpse of them, but by the time we reach adulthood, most of us are so hedged about with inhibitions, self-doubt and self-dislike that these glimpses are all too rare. So what happens in between?

Falling from grace

We have children for all sorts of reasons, and we load upon them all sorts of dreams and projections, whether we know it or not. Some are personal: 'Be what I never managed to be', 'Follow in your father's footsteps', 'Love me unconditionally', and so on. Others are cultural, and are often taken for granted; 'Don't show your feelings', for example, is something that a lot of English people take on board, but it is by no means universal – thank goodness – to the rest of the human race.

And as the child grows and his or her own uniqueness becomes more obvious, conflict arises. You can't be all that your parents want you to be, however hard you try. And with that realisation comes the first blow to self-esteem. If my mother doesn't find me beautiful just the way I am, then I am not beautiful. In order to be beautiful, I have to change. I have to become less noisy, more obedient, eat what I'm given, be polite to people I don't like, and so on. The list goes on, and there are endless variations on the theme, but the message the child gleans is the same: I am not all right as I am.

It doesn't matter how gentle or enlightened the parents are, or how carefully they try to foster the child's spirit. None of us reaches adulthood without some damage to our self-esteem, and it is part of the work of adulthood to reclaim it. The process of socialisation makes us smaller. We are getting messages all the time, firstly from our parents and other caretakers, and later from siblings, friends, teachers and the wider world around us: messages that say, whether subtly or directly, 'This is okay. That is not okay'. As a result we cut ourselves down to size, close down parts of ourselves that do not meet with approval, and grow up to be functioning adults, operating from a tiny part of the potential that we were born with.

The price that we pay for conformity is direct and simple. *As you stop being yourself, you stop liking yourself.* To the extent that you sacrifice your truth, so you also cease to feel love for yourself, even though your mother or your classmates or whoever is assuring you that you are far more lovable when you behave as they want you to behave. And with self-love goes ease of self-expression, the capacity for joy and the ability to make mistakes, to take in and let go.

Quite a few of the stories in this chapter are drawn from long-term therapy groups, because rebuilding self-esteem is something you can't do alone. You need friends to hold up positive mirrors to you when you can't see your own beauty; you need them along the way, to witness the changes you make, support you through tough times and celebrate your successes. In an ideal world, everyone would have friends like these, and I would be out of a job – but the groups I run are a kind of training ground for learning the skills you need to be able to create and maintain genuine and lasting friendships.

An interesting example is that of Nigel, who came to one of my year-long training groups. Nigel's problem seemed to be a sort of 'superiority complex'; rather than having low self-esteem, he seemed to feel that other people, on the whole, were not good enough for him. He came from a wealthy family and had inherited a great deal of money in his own right, together with a beautiful house and land. Despite his good connections and material advantages, however, he was not happy. His relationships with women had always been short-term, because sooner or later his current partner would fail to live up to his expectations. Friendships were also a disaster, for similar reasons.

Committing himself to a long-term therapy group was an act of great courage for Nigel. It was not long before he found himself challenged on all sides, for to the other group members he appeared arrogant, aloof, lacking in feeling for others and unwilling to give of himself. There were times when I thought that he would leave the group, but his armour was so strong that challenges seemed simply to bounce off, leaving him unmoved. It was several months before he began, slowly and painfully, to open up.

What emerged was that, from babyhood onwards, a strong sense of his own importance had been instilled in him. He was special, he was different – but not because of any quality in himself. His importance, his worth as a human being, lay in the fact that he was an inheritor. One day, a great deal of family wealth and property would be his. Almost daily, it seemed, his father had alluded to this in some way, and impressed upon him that this placed him a cut above other people.

Nigel had inherited this belief along with his wealth, but the shadow side of the legacy, of which he himself was only half aware, was a total lack of appreciation for himself, Nigel, simply for being who he was. He had never been seen, let alone loved or valued, just as himself. How could he possibly even begin to know what was missing? It followed that most of the people he met in the course of his life had also been blinded by his status, and had been unable to see beyond it – or had not cared enough to try. In the group, however, Nigel was forced, again and again, to witness the pain of others and to stay with their bewilderment and anger as they bruised themselves against his defences. Eventually, his own pain became too great, and the defences began to slip. Behind them, behind the mask of Nigel the inheritor, was a lonely, frightened, desperate little boy who had no idea how to go about the business of loving and being loved, let alone any sense that he deserved it.

Here is where the alchemy of group support begins to work. As the other group members began to be able to see his pain, his anger, and also the delightful child that he had once been, so they began to warm towards him. Nigel began to experience real liking from others, for the first time in his adult life. As he allowed it in, his defences softened further.

By the end of the year, when the group broke up, he had made four or five friends with whom he stayed in contact. They were able to support him in beginning to dismantle some of the self-destructive behaviour patterns that he had built up as a way to deaden his pain, and which eloquently expressed his lack of love for himself. The most urgent of these was his heavy and habitual drinking, which had grown from being a natural part of his lifestyle to an addiction. He could not break it on his own, and with no strong and loving relationships in his life, he had had no reason to do so. Now, however, instead of helping him to cope, it began to get in the way. Through receiving love from others, Nigel began to be able to love himself, and to want to care for himself better.

With support from his friends, and from myself as his therapist, Nigel went into a residential clinic dealing with alcoholism and other dependencies, where he knew he would be intensively challenged, and unable to avoid facing the issues which the alcohol was masking. He stayed there for several weeks, going through a kind of rebirth, stripping away the layers of the identity that he had inherited, and had built upon, for most of his life.

When Nigel came out, he was in an almost unbearably raw and vulnerable state, but with a dawning sense of choice in the way that he approached the world, and of responsibility to himself – first and foremost – in the choices that he made. Of course, he came up against immense pressure, especially from his family, to take up where he had left off, but with his new and growing self-respect, and the affirmation of his trusted friends, he was able to keep open the space for a more loving, and lovable, self to emerge.

Counting the cost

When it comes to making relationships, low self-esteem is an enormous handicap. You make poor choices, you give up too easily or refuse to let go and you sabotage the flow of love in all sorts of ways, if only to give yourself the sour triumph of proving, once again, that you're just not worth it. People tend to gravitate towards others whose self-esteem is at a similar level, so that on the whole, you get exactly what you think you deserve. A relationship between someone whose self-esteem is high and someone who has low self-esteem is unlikely to survive, if indeed it ever gets off the ground in the first place. As a friend of mine put it, 'I went looking for a goddess, but when I found her, she was looking for a god.'

Of course, there are plenty of ways in which we try to convince ourselves and other people that we're really just fine, thank you. We wear masks most of the time; masks that we've learned, one way or another, will get us approval or liking or some kind of positive attention. Some are designed to achieve the opposite effect, to make us less noticeable. The masks say to the world: 'This is who I am. I am a nice person. I care for others. I make people laugh. I am a success in my work. I am attractive, sexy, dynamic. Please, look no further.' As my friend and fellow therapist Leo Rutherford is fond of saying, 'I'm fine' really stands for 'I'm Fucked Up, Insecure, Neurotic and Emotionally Unstable!'

There's nothing wrong with masks, they are an essential part of our lives, but when we use them to deny the deeper reality beneath, then we are in trouble. If we cannot take them off sometimes, we cannot really touch and be touched. I remember Jim, who came to one of my five-day groups and entertained us all with his razor-sharp wit. For the first three days I was delightfully amused by him. The mask was a work of art; it took me that long to see that his humour kept everyone at arm's length, and shielded him from his own feelings. Beneath it was a deep well of sadness and despair. It was only when the mask was removed and he was able to allow himself to feel liked – and hence likable – in this vulnerable state, that he could begin to see that he need not wear it all the time. The relief was incredible. Until we take our courage in both hands and unmask in this way, we cannot appreciate what an immense effort it is to keep smiling, to maintain the charade.

Often, you can hide your self-hatred even from yourself. It is hard work, desperately hard, to keep it all together and convince yourself and the rest of the world that you're okay, you're making it as a human being, if behind the bright facade is the secret knowledge of your own worthlessness, but it can be done. Millions of us do it every day.

It works quite well until something comes along that is outside your control, something that breaks down your carefully built structures and lets in the forces of chaos. This can be losing your job, ending a relationship, a quarrel with a friend or even just the washing machine breaking down – it only depends upon the thickness of the veneer. Where someone with a healthy self-regard would rage or grieve, and then muster their resources to meet the situation, you are suddenly immobilised, stopped in your tracks by the uprush of despair and self-loathing, the voice that says, 'I'm no good. There's no point in anything.'

How to get help

There are plenty of ways to avoid getting love and support when you need it; most of us are highly skilled at deflecting our friends' concern, and often we don't even realise we are doing it. Here's a story that you might find familiar.

Peter was a counsellor and had cast himself in a largely supportive role to his friends as well. He tended to be seen by others as strong, solid, gentle and trustworthy. He didn't say much, as a rule, yet this clearly stemmed from difficulty in expressing himself rather than from a state of peace and serenity.

We were at a peer group meeting of about a dozen people. Many of us hadn't met for a while, and there was a happy, lively atmosphere. However, Peter was obviously upset about something, though he tried not to let it show. When someone asked what was the matter, he tried very hard to turn the attention away from himself, saying that he did not want to stop other people from having a good time. This is one of the tricks you can use to stop yourself from getting help in climbing out of the pit of despair; you imagine that you will somehow infect others with your own darkness. In fact, as Peter found, your friends can't help being aware of it at some level, and it affects them insidiously, indirectly. Far from becoming a burden to them, it is usually a huge relief to them as well as to you to bring it out into the open.

Peter's next argument was that it would be more painful for him to talk about, or express, his feelings, than it was to keep them under wraps. Not surprisingly, this did not cut much ice with the rest of us. Once you have broken through this barrier for yourself, and experienced the sense of lightness and new energy that it brings, this particular defence begins to lose its power.

He also feared that 'If I allow myself to open up here, among people who can understand these things, then I only have to go back into the outside world, and it will be worse then because I'll be feeling, and I won't have the support.' This fear is a real one, in that once you begin to allow yourself to feel, it becomes much harder to close down again. However, the solution is to go about setting up the support in the 'outside world' as well, rather than keeping the lid firmly shut and refusing to honour your own needs. There are always friends who will be more than willing to listen. To deny yourself support is yet another form of self-sabotage.

Faced with our refusal to leave him alone with his misery, Peter was bewildered. What had he done to deserve so much loving attention? The answer, of course, was nothing. You don't have to do anything at all to deserve time and care from others – or from yourself. For Peter, this was the turning point. It made him think that if all those people thought that he was worth bothering with, then maybe he was. When you truly can't find it in you to love and care for yourself, the first step towards healing is to allow yourself to receive love from other people.

Peter wept, a few difficult tears. For him at that point, it was a major step in self-exposure and trust. It takes time to digest and take on board new experiences; you have to allow enough space for them to become integrated into your life. Sometimes change can be revolutionary, but more often it happens slowly, step by step, as you gain the courage to take small risks and challenge the habits of a lifetime.

At our next meeting, Peter was the first to speak, rather than the last. He revealed more of himself as he spoke, and this in turn changed the way we responded to him. People felt him to be more trustworthy, simply because they could see him better. The caring, supportive stance that had been his refuge was not lost; instead, his relationships within the group took on a new vitality as the possibility of both give and take began to emerge.

So, take a risk. Choose a friend, someone you trust; if you've done any of the previous exercises in this book, you've already got several candidates for the job. Be honest about what's going on for you, and invite your friend to be honest in return. Everyone finds things tough sometimes, and it helps to talk. It helps even more if having a good time is also on the agenda! This says, 'Crying on someone's shoulder is not the main point of friendship. It's a way of dealing with painful things and getting support, but it's only a step on the path towards enjoying life in the company of good friends.' So try to build in something positive to do as well.

Exercise 7
Opening up

STEP 1
Set up your private space with your partner or with a friend. As in the exercise on page 42, one of you will talk and the other will listen. This time, use your five minutes to talk about something you are finding difficult in your life at the moment. Talk about yourself, about what *you* are feeling. What frightens you or keeps you awake at night? What are you ashamed of?

STEP 2
When it is your turn to listen, try to be present without judgment. Show by your attention that you are there for your friend.

Be ready to meet their eyes when they look at you. Notice your breathing; you may hold your breath, or breathe more quickly and shallowly, if you are finding something challenging. Keep it as slow and even as you can, and it will help you to stay present. Your friend is taking a big risk in opening up to you in this way. The chances are that you will feel sympathy and understanding rather than shock and disgust. Let your friend see this. At the end, thank them for confiding in you.

STEP 3

Thank each other and move on. You may decide together that you want to go on talking outside the structure of the exercise, or you may choose to do something else, something that celebrates the intimacy you have shared – go out to meet other friends, have a meal, go to the cinema; whatever you fancy.

Note: if your friend or your partner tells you things that are really disturbing or shocking to you, they will be aware of your response at some level, so you must acknowledge it within the exercise after they have finished speaking. They are giving you the gift of trust and this may take some courage on their part; make sure you reward it rather than judging or shaming. They need your honest response; if this has been too big for them to bear alone, the exercise is a first step towards getting support. Tell them if you feel out of your depth; maybe some other form of help would be appropriate, and you can offer to support them in getting it. Take some time to digest what you have heard, and make sure you have another meeting set up when you feel able to respond in a way that honours them for what they have shared.

One change leads to another, making it progressively harder for you to hold on to your old patterns. With hindsight, of course, the rewards that follow this kind of risk-taking far outweigh the fears of ridicule or rejection that you carry, but the first step is always the hardest. The fear is real. A kind of death awaits you, the death of the persona with which you have faced the world up to now, and it is appropriate to be afraid.

The discipline of self-love

People often think that it is somehow self-indulgent to look after themselves. On the contrary: it demands practice and discipline, and continued vigilance to make sure that the time, space and nourishment that we all deserve in our lives do not get eroded away by the demands of work, home and those around us.

There's an element of self-discipline, too, in the task of rooting out negative feelings about yourself. They don't serve you in any way; they get between you and your aliveness, your experience of your own beauty and that of other people, yet you cling to them, you indulge yourself in them. It is painful to be useless, stupid, ugly or whatever your particular putdown may be, but it is a safe, familiar pain. The process of regrowing yourself is a slow one. It is seldom dramatic, and often difficult and disruptive as you outgrow the limitations that were all you thought you deserved.

Exercise 8
Throwing out rubbish

This one can be done with one person, as before, or in a group. The more witnesses you have, the more powerful it can be, but do not push yourself into a situation that will make you feel uncomfortable.

STEP 1

Each person chooses some quality or way of behaving that they wish to leave behind, which does not serve them any longer. It could be one of the things you talked about in the last exercise, or something else you want to walk away from. Make sure it is small and specific enough to be manageable; don't set yourself up to fail. People choose all kinds of things to throw away – 'my inner critic', 'my anger with my ex-partner', 'my addiction to chocolate' are a few that come to mind. Write it on a piece of paper, or choose some object that symbolises what you want to get rid of.

STEP 2

Come together in the place you have chosen. You can decide in advance how to dispose of your 'rubbish'. Burning it is a good choice, indoors or outside. Burying it or throwing it into the sea or a river are other possibilities. Each person in turn speaks about what they are throwing away. When it is your turn, speak with passion; this is a piece of theatre, but it really can make a difference if you put your heart into it. As each person lets go of whatever it is, everyone else applauds.

STEP 3

Celebrate! You just got rid of some of the useless baggage that weighs you down. This is one of the first steps to self-healing. You might need to do it more than once, but each time a space is opened up in your life and you get a glimpse of what life might be like without being driven by negative thoughts and habits. Each time, their hold on you will be loosened a little.

The healing journey

The work of change, then, is a gradual process. It begins with noticing what you do to sell yourself short or put yourself down and recognising that, as an adult, you create your own life. Whatever you were taught as a child, it could not possibly encompass the immense potential that you carry within you.

You have a choice: to stay within the boundaries that you were given, or take responsibility for yourself and create your own. Paradoxically, those of us who have been most gravely hurt in childhood are those most likely to break free from the old limitations and widen their choices for themselves. Pain provides the impetus. Changes come about as a by-product of exploring the areas of damage, and as these inner changes begin to happen, so you become able to make changes, through conscious choice, in your outer life as well.

Reparenting yourself

When you can't care for yourself enough, you look to others to do it for you. Usually unconsciously, you search for someone to be for you what your parents could not be: always there, always loving, never letting you down.

The bad news is that this search is doomed. Until you learn how to be mother and father to yourself, the child within will continue to reach out to anyone who gets close enough. Sooner or later this child, with its desperate neediness, its unreasoning demands and its inability to see anyone else's point of view, will be hurt again; and again. Before you can truly love and be loved by others, you have to learn to look after yourself, to give yourself what your parents could not or would not give you.

As you learn, as you begin to act from a place of strength rather than from your pain, what you expect from relationships changes. When you look at those close to you, partners or friends or parents or children, you see with clear eyes. You see not your own projections, but other human beings, able to meet you in some ways, and not so able in others. When arrows are fired at you, you begin to be able to see that you don't have to be wounded, that the person wielding the weapons is acting from his or her own pain. Eventually, compassion grows. And when appreciation comes your way, you no longer side-step it like a matador dodging the charge of a bull; you allow it in, you accept it as your due.

Exercise 9
Singing your own praises

STEP 1
Sit down with your partner or a friend, as before. Like Exercise 8, this can also be done with a group of friends. This time, take your five minutes to tell your friends or partner about all your good qualities, the things you like about yourself. Tell stories about things you have done that you feel proud of.

Avoid making lists; if you see yourself as compassionate, for example, talk about a time when you have really felt yourself to own this quality.

Five minutes can feel like forever! We have strong taboos about 'blowing our own trumpets', and it can feel very dangerous, courting retribution. Make sure you don't negate what you're saying – as in 'I'm very methodical in my work – well, I try to be, anyway . . .'. Try to stay conscious and really mean what you are saying, but don't be afraid of silence as well. Take the time to let your thoughts form. And notice how the others are responding. One fear is that they will think you are 'above yourself', 'too big for your boots', and so on. This is playground stuff, and it is time to leave it behind.

STEP 2
As you listen, notice how difficult it can be for people to do this exercise. Some will try to distance themselves by giving a grand performance; others will giggle, hide their faces or run out of things to say. Just listen, and be supportive. You are all in the same boat.

STEP 3
At the end of each person's turn, give them some applause. They may need a reassuring hug as well! Then, when everyone has finished, find a way to celebrate together.

Loving ourselves: four levels of being

The work of rebuilding and reclaiming goes on at many levels. For the sake of clarity, it is helpful to look at people in terms of four realms – the body, the emotions, the mind and the spirit – while recognising that you can't cut up human beings in real life, and that what happens in one part of you inevitably affects the other parts as well. We also need to be conscious of the hierarchy implicit in this view, in that we tend to regard the physical as the 'lowest' level and the spiritual as the 'highest', and do ourselves a grave injustice in the process. With these cautions in mind, we can begin to look at how low self-esteem affects us at each of these levels, and what we can do to change this.

THE BODY

On the first level, that of the body, our love or lack of love for ourselves is at its most visible. It's not hard to see when someone is not at ease in their body. The way they move, their clothes – trying too hard, or not hard enough – the way they speak and express themselves, all tell the story. Because we are taught to see the body as the lowest part of our being, it is an easy focus for self-hatred. We use and abuse it, ignoring the messages it gives about its true wants and needs. Eventually, our health begins to suffer in one way or another.

Here is an invitation to wake up and begin the work of healing; you can choose either to try to suppress the symptoms and carry on along your chosen path, or to stop and take the time to ask yourself why this is happening. What can you do to change it? Suppressing or ignoring symptoms tends to lead to further breakdown, more loss of life force. We can, quite literally, allow ourselves to die through lack of self-love.

I am not suggesting that we are to blame for all our bodily ills – thinking in that way ends up as yet another form of self-punishment – but that we owe it to ourselves to take responsibility for the way we are, and to take the appropriate action. What that action may be depends, of course, on the individual, but its roots are to be found in the part of us that says, I am worth looking after. I deserve better than this. The rest is down to good, solid support, a measure of faith in results that may not be immediately obvious, and the discipline to keep noticing, keep coming back to the new path, until old, self-destructive habits finally begin to loosen their hold. Anyone who has been through the process of giving up smoking or dieting to lose weight will understand what this means.

Exercise 10
Loving your body

STEP 1

Meet with your partner or your chosen friend in the usual way. Again, if you like, you can do this exercise with a small group of friends. This time, use your five minutes to speak about your body. How well do you look after yourself? Think about the things you do that you know are not good for you. It could be something obvious, like smoking, drinking too much or food abuse. Or it could be something more subtle, like not bothering to eat proper meals or not exercising enough (or too much). Do you take care over what you wear and how you look?

STEP 2

When each of you has spoken, go around again. This time, choose one thing to focus on – something you are unhappy about and feel that you can change. With the help of your partner – who is allowed to speak if asked – make your way towards a specific intention. Make sure it is something achievable – 'I am going to lose weight' is not much use, but 'I will eat three meals a day with no snacks in between for five days' might be. At the end of the five days, you can reward yourself – though not with food! – and renew your intention, if you like, for the next five days. Positive intentions are better than negative ones – so 'I will dress to impress at work next week' is better than 'I will stop being a slob'. And the reward is important; your partner can help to decide what it should be. Have some fun with this bit!

STEP 3

After an agreed length of time in which you have both agreed to carry out your intentions, meet again and check in with each other. In between, even if you live together, try not to comment on what your partner is or is not doing – except for giving them plenty of appreciation if they are sticking to the plan. When you meet, talk about how things have been, and how you felt about yourself when you succeeded, and when (if) you failed. Give each other constructive feedback, and formulate a new intention for the next time period.

Together with the other members of one of my long-term groups, I witnessed this process happening for Dorothy, a woman in her thirties. She had always been 'big', and she had built this into her persona, as people often do, so that it became linked with the qualities of warmth, generosity and openness; qualities which she prized about herself. The dark side, the hidden price that is paid by so many women in our culture, with its narrow and – for most women – unattainable standards of beauty and attractiveness, was that she did not feel beautiful or worthy of being loved by others. Certainly, she did not love herself as she was, and her secret shame about her body made her unable to meet other people on an equal footing.

Dorothy had been in therapy for some months, and as she began to open up some of the places where she had been wounded, to begin the work of healing and of looking after herself, so her self-esteem began to improve. One of the things that she really began to enjoy was movement and dancing as one way to express the new creativity and zest for life that was rising within her. However, she became increasingly frustrated with the inability of her body to do what she wanted it to do – 'I really want to be able to move freely and lose myself in the dancing, but my body just won't let me.' Witnessed by the group, she declared her intention to shed some of the weight she was carrying.

During the course of the year, we kept company with Dorothy as she carried out her intention, changing lifelong habits and dealing with the emotional revolutions as the fat began to disappear. By the time of our final meeting she had lost about five stone, and felt and looked completely different. Here was a woman who was proud of herself, who knew that she was worth looking after. The weight loss had happened – and this is a very important point, the key to understanding why so many diets fail – not as an end in itself, but as a by-product of her rising self-esteem. Rather than serving any purpose, her excess weight now got in the way. At our last meeting, Dorothy danced, ecstatically, beautifully. Watching her, watching the joy and vitality shining out through her dance, I was moved to tears.

Loving our feelings

Dorothy's story leads us on to the level of the emotions and of self-expression, for our ability to look after ourselves physically has its roots in emotional well-being. The most obvious examples of this are the ways in which we can use food, tobacco, alcohol and so forth as a direct means to suppress our emotions and dull our pain.

Lack of self-esteem shows up on the emotional level as a lack of *joie de vivre*, a basic zest for life. This leads on to depression, emotional greyness and ultimately despair. How do you feel when you wake up in the morning? Can you shout when you feel like it, cry your eyes out or laugh your head off? Can you play like a child, make mistakes and let them go? How do you express yourself creatively? Creativity is an essential part of being human, and a person who is not creative is in pain, is suffering from the loss of self-love. It doesn't have to be painting or playing the piano or 'making' in the obvious sense, just some way in which what you do expresses something of your truth.

When I lived in London, I used to travel to work every day on the 74 bus. I always made a point of trying to catch the 8.45. The conductor was a middle-aged, genial, bearded chap, who created a magical environment on his bus. Each passenger was made to feel special, from little old ladies to po-faced businessmen. His sense of humour was electric, and never malicious. A sense of merriment pervaded the journey, and I always got off feeling recharged. In his ordinary way, that bus conductor was being extraordinarily creative, and touching many lives with brightness.

Once again, the road back to self-love involves noticing what you are doing, forming the intention to change it, and then bringing that intention into reality. As Dorothy found, it takes time, continued attention and loving support. Making time and space to be creative can be hard if your life is full of other, apparently more important commitments, but it must be done, for your life's sake. One step leads to another, and it is a process that becomes easier and faster as you begin to give yourself the message that you are worth it.

Exercise 11
Expressing yourself

STEP 1

Set up your time and place as usual, with one or more trusted friends. In this exercise, we will focus not so much on expressing emotions – which is dealt with in Chapter 5 – but on expressing yourself creatively. What do you do in your life that you really put something of yourself into? It could be your work, it could be sports or some other activity. It could be learning something, or it could be singing or dancing, painting or performing. What you must not include here is your children. Although bringing up children is one of the greatest things you can undertake in your life, they are not your creations. Besides, being a parent is often a reason why your creativity gets submerged – in the intensity and exhaustion of it all, especially in the early years, keeping some space for yourself can get pushed off the agenda.

You may find that you do feel fulfilled in this way, that your creative life is rich and satisfying. If so, allow yourself some self-congratulation. It takes effort and continuous vigilance to look after yourself in this way. However, there may be things you've always wanted to do but never found the time for them, or maybe you used to be good at something and it has somehow got left behind. Check your feelings; when you hear a friend talking about the art class they go to or how exciting their work is, do you feel a twinge of envy? If so, there is something missing. Use this space to explore what it may be.

STEP 2

In this exercise, you may want to move into conversation, giving each other suggestions, helping to uncover your secret dreams or think up new ones. It could be that you find your way to a joint project, going to a class or a concert together, or even going on holiday. If you are doing the exercise with your partner, it could include decorating your home, but be careful that it does not become more of a chore than a pleasure. Keep checking how you feel; you will know when you find the right thing.

STEP 3

Finish by speaking your intentions to each other, with a time limit by which you will have at least made a beginning. Ask each other's help to make sure you succeed; the flip side of low self-esteem is a sort of arrogance that would rather fail than admit to needing help. And give each other constructive feedback; arrange to meet again soon, and talk about how it feels to be carrying out your plans.

Once again, support, in the form of loving friends or possibly therapy, is essential. This work cannot be done alone. Low self-esteem flourishes in isolation, fed by the original wounding that cut us off from ourselves and from other people. The way back lies in speaking and being heard, in expressing our 'negative' feelings and being received. In the people around us we have mirrors that will show us how we are doing, whether we inspire love and affection, whether we are valued for our own uniqueness. Self-expression needs to be witnessed, and from self-love flows joy in the company of true friends.

THE MIND

Moving on now to the level of the mind, we find that lack of self-esteem can manifest itself in various ways. A common result of wounding in childhood is for a person to become cynical, unable to show enthusiasm, putting down other people in order to feel safe and in control. Or he or she may be cautious and unconfident in their thinking, afraid to pursue ideas for fear of ridicule, and unable to believe that their ideas could have any value in any case. In the extreme, someone who has been badly hurt may turn their rage and fear outwards, looking for a relatively safe place to vent these feelings, and this leads to intolerance, narrow-mindedness and bigotry. At the root of prejudice is pain.

Another common way in which low self-esteem can show up is in mental 'cleverness', intellect without heart. Cleverness is generally approved of in our culture, and it can enable one to attain some of the goals that we are taught to strive for, such as money, success and power. Many of us are driven to try too hard here, feeling that if only we can 'make it' in the eyes of the world, we will be all right. Unfortunately, the goalposts tend to keep moving, and however successful we may become, the starving child within remains as hungry as ever.

The same is true for those of us who retreat into the mind as a refuge from feeling, living in our heads and doing our best to deny our pain. The pain is still there, even if we cannot feel it, and the head is a poor place from which to conduct relationships.

I am reminded here of Isabel, a woman in her forties who took part in a year-long group. Her insights were acute, but she used them like javelins, knowing just where to aim to hurt most. Hers was a clarity without kindness, a piercing vision, and people tended to avoid engaging with her once they had learned that they invariably came off the worst in any encounter. She held power, certainly, and she commanded respect, but it was a lonely place to be.

Isabel's position in the group accurately reflected the way she had set things up in the world 'outside', and it showed her very clearly how arid her emotional and spiritual life had become. What fuelled her mental sharpness was despair born of pain carried for many years and never shared. Once she had taken up her position and driven everyone off to a safe distance with her barbed comments, she could not then reach out when she needed to and break through the defences that she had created.

During the long summer break, Isabel decided to go on a prolonged spiritual retreat. Here, in silence and solitude, backed up by guidance and support when she needed it, she found the nourishment and easing of pain for which she was seeking.

When the group came together again in the autumn, we noticed an astonishing change in her. The quality of her presence was no less powerful, but in a very different way. She had become both stronger and softer, with a new humility that enabled her to offer her insights in such a way that they could be received gladly, and so, in turn, to receive what came to her from others.

Generally speaking, as Isabel came to understand, the way to look after your mind is to look first to your emotional and spiritual health. The intellect is fed by free creativity and by the openness and lively curiosity that follow from emotional well-being, and it is kept in balance by a strong connection with spirit.

On the practical, everyday level, you can be discriminating in what you choose to take in, whether through reading, films and television, theatre and so on, or through the company you keep. Again, the question can be asked, does this nourish you? Do you need to read the newspapers if they simply feed your despair? Is it good for you to be with people whose thinking you find uncongenial? If you take the time to ask the question, the answer is usually clear, and then you can make a conscious choice, honouring yourself in the process.

THE SPIRIT

On the last level, that of the spirit, low self-esteem reduces your ability to touch and be touched. You lose the sense of something greater than yourself; awe, wonder and reverence are removed from the spectrum of your feelings. How can you feel confident that you are part of the divine scheme of things, life's celebration of itself, if you are convinced that you are just not good enough?

For many of us, the pain of this exile from the realm of spirit is so great that we try to deal with it by denying the reality of the sacred altogether, and take refuge in the mind or in the myriad diversions that the world offers. There's a paradox here, in that it is pain – through crisis, grief, and loss of hope – that very often forces us to look beyond ourselves, to open to spirit once again. When we recognise that we cannot cope on our own, we have begun the work of healing. Isabel's story is a good example of this process at work.

The particular road that you take is not that important; what matters is whether it is a path with heart. Again, if you are part of a religious community or church, you can ask yourself whether it truly strengthens your connection with the divine? Is your soul nourished here? Can your fellow travellers be with you in your grief, your vulnerability, your celebration? If not, what are you doing here?

Equally, some form of spiritual practice helps to recall us to ourselves when we lose the way, and keeps the channel open for the flow of joy and wonder in our lives. It need not be formal prayer or meditation; there are countless ways to commune with spirit, from being alone in nature to playing football. Whatever takes you out of yourself, brings you into the present moment, and leaves you feeling refreshed and at peace, will feed your spirit. Without some space for this in your life, your spirit will starve.

Exercise 12
Celebrating yourselves together

STEP 1
Meet your partner at your chosen time and place. This time, only one of you is going to speak; the other will have their turn another time. Imagine that you are going first.

You are going to outline the evening of your choice, and your partner will make it happen. You can ask for whatever you want – within realistic limits, of course – and there will be no compromise; the night is yours. Allow yourself to imagine what you'd really like to do, where to go, who to see. For once, you deserve to have exactly what you want; you've worked hard to get this far, and this is your reward. Don't hold back; remember that your partner will have their turn in due course. Have some fun with this one!

There is only one proviso. This is not about sex; there will be scope for that later. Sometimes sex can get in the way of intimacy, so for now, focus on having a good time together in other ways. This is about treating yourself, being special and being honoured as such.

STEP 2
Make sure that you agree on a time when your partner will have their turn. If you enjoy yourselves, do it again – as many times as you like.

What next?

In this chapter, we have looked at how lack of love for yourself can stop you forming good relationships, and how this begins. We've looked at some ways to heal your self-esteem, and seen that this inevitably involves taking risks with other people, showing them how you feel. In other words, as you work on your self-esteem, you can't help becoming more intimate with others as well – and not just with one partner, but with a number of friends. So, in looking after yourself, you are also looking after your closest relationships. In the next chapter, we go on to look at one of the biggest problem areas in relationship: feelings, and how to handle them.

Chapter 5

Expressing Your Feelings – the Heartland of Relationship

To laugh is to risk appearing the fool.

To weep is to risk appearing sentimental.

To reach out is to risk involvement.

To expose feelings is to risk exposing your true self.

To place your ideas and dreams before the crowd is
to risk their love.

To love is to risk not being loved in return.

To live is to risk dying.

To hope is to risk despair.

To try is to risk failure.

But the greatest hazard in life is to risk nothing.

The one who risks nothing does nothing and has
nothing – and finally is nothing.

He may avoid sufferings and sorrow,

But he simply cannot learn, feel, change, grow or
love.

Chained by his certitude, he is a slave; he has
forfeited freedom.

Only one who risks is free.

Anon

We come now to the place where we fight our fiercest battles and attain our closest intimacy. For a relationship to work, for it to be nourishing for both partners, there must be a strong emotional meeting. That does not mean perfect harmony; in fact, quite the reverse. It means a willingness to be real with one another, to feel whatever you are feeling, and to deal with whatever responses there may be. If you can stay with that, then you have a chance of winning through to genuine closeness, true intimacy, a place that lies way beyond the apparent closeness of being in love.

Why is it so hard for us to do this? The answer is to be found on two levels, both in the here and now, and in the past. Ultimately, though, it springs from a single source: the fear that if you show who you really are, you will be rejected, not received, not loved. If you want to be loved, you must never take off your mask.

The present: what if they don't like me?

Picture the scene in the early days of what you hope will become an intimate relationship. You are anxious to impress, to be seen in the best light. Already in love or well on the way there, you are viewing your would-be lover through a golden glow, and automatically discounting their less than wonderful qualities. If something upsets or irritates you, you hold your tongue, not wanting to dispel the magic – and it works, for a while. But as the magic begins to seep away, these minor irritations start to grow in importance. Some of them may become major stumbling blocks. What happens next?

Here the road divides. If you have already learned something about expressing your emotions gracefully, and with respect for the other person, then you are well on the way to creating a viable partnership. If not, then the first real row may demolish the fragile structure that you have begun to build. Feelings that have been held in have a way of attaching themselves to something trivial – like the legendary toothpaste tube – and spilling out clumsily, wounding those whom you love, shocking you out of your fond illusions, and destroying trust, perhaps forever. If you are used to hiding your feelings, then the next step, after conflict has arisen, is to try to hide your hurt as well. Not wanting to make yourself vulnerable to this other person who has wounded you, you retreat; then so the distance between the two of you grows.

There is the third way, the way of continued suppression. Partnerships where 'difficult' emotions are simply not handled can last a long time – perhaps a lifetime – although the cost is high in terms of aliveness. Along with the free flow of rage and tears, you also lose your joy and your passion. There is always the risk, too, that you will meet someone else who will call out these buried feelings, all the more intensely because they have been denied expression for too long.

The story of my client, Tom, illustrates this only too well. Tom had been married for nineteen years to Carrie, and together they had brought up three children. It was a good, solid, respectable marriage, and all seemed well. Then Tom became friendly with one of his wife's friends, Sarah, attracted by what he described as her 'craziness' and ability to enjoy life. They began a wild affair, and he discovered in himself an enormous sense of fun that had never found expression in his marriage. He left his wife, then tried to return, torn between his love for her and the children and his new sense of himself.

The return was a failure, for although Carrie too yearned for more fun in her life, somehow they could not rekindle the spark between them. Tom now lives with Sarah, and his children no longer speak to him. Some way along the road, the same problems are beginning to crop up with Sarah that he encountered with Carrie, and they are not having fun any more.

The message in this cautionary tale is a stark one: unless you learn to know what you feel, whether 'good' or 'bad', and to communicate it honestly, you are condemned to follow the same patterns again and again.

Where do these patterns come from? To answer this question, we need to look at how we take our first steps in learning to handle our emotions.

The past: paradise lost

Somewhere in early childhood, you begin to learn the art of hiding what you really feel. The emotions of a young child are strong, vivid and immediate. She cannot contain her grief, her joy, her rage; she cannot postpone it until a more convenient moment, or express just enough for those around her to cope with. But strong emotions evoke strong reactions, particularly in adults who learned, in their turn, to push their feelings down. Usually, the so-called 'negative' feelings are the ones they have trouble with. Anger, fear and grief stand at the top of the list. Sexuality takes its place here too. And there are other emotions, not usually labelled 'negative', which are often sanctioned, subtly or not so subtly: the expression of excitement, joy, or enthusiasm, for instance. Each of us could make our own personal list.

The reactions of adults may vary from subtle disapproval to outright physical violence, but the message that we get as children is the same: it is not all right to feel this way, or to show that we feel this way. As a result we cut ourselves down to size as best we can – and we survive.

What happens to the feelings that we suppress? They don't just depart, never to darken our doors again. As long as we are alive – and this is a blessing, not a curse – there is something in our being that is continually striving for wholeness. The suppressed feelings wait, just beyond the threshold. Sometimes they seep in under the door and through the keyhole. When our attention is drawn that way, we hear them knocking for admittance. Sometimes, when we are in crisis or the effort of keeping it all in check simply becomes too great, they break down the door and erupt into our lives, causing chaos.

We do right to fear these unwanted guests, for they threaten the order that we work so hard to maintain. Suppression lends them energy; they grow stronger and darker, with far greater destructive potential than they ever had in the first place. People who come into therapy are often terrified of their own pent-up feelings, particularly anger. They imagine that if they give vent to their rage, they may destroy themselves or other people. There is no doubt that many acts of violence are fuelled by intense emotions, but I am pleased to say that in my experience, nothing so catastrophic has ever happened in a therapeutic situation. Instead, the time bomb is defused, and the relief of finally giving up control is immense. The energy invested in suppression, and the power that these banished spectres hold, can return to where they rightfully belong. We will look at some examples of how this happens below.

The feelings that give us most trouble fall into four types: fear, anger, grief and sexuality. I have also mentioned enthusiasm, joy and passion, but it is my experience that there is less need to work on these directly, for as we feel our way back into our so-called 'negative' emotions, so we regain our ability to have and to express the more 'positive' ones as well. Each of these four types of feeling, if not felt or not expressed spontaneously as they arise, will colour our lives, and limit our ability to relate to others in various ways. Sexuality is the province of Chapter 7; the first three are explored below.

Facing our fears

What do you do when you are afraid? At the simplest level, there are three kinds of response. Suppose, for instance, that you are suddenly faced with a dangerous wild animal – probably the most likely thing that our fear responses were evolved to cope with. You might scream and run for your life, and this would be an active expression of your terror. Or you might freeze, unable to move, which would be a passive response. Or the third way, if you were able to ride the fear and use the rush of adrenalin to help clear your thinking and speed up your reflexes, might be to find some unexpected strategy to save yourself – climbing a tree, perhaps, or throwing dirt in the monster's eyes.

All of these possibilities have some survival value, depending on the circumstances, but it is obvious that being able to keep your head and not go into a blind panic can only be a good thing. There are two points to be made here. One is that unless you are used to facing fear, working with it and seeing beyond it, you don't have that third option. You can only go with your instinctive gut reaction. The other is that the ability to 'keep your head' when you are afraid comes with experience and emotional maturity. Some adults can manage it some of the time, but a young child cannot do it at all.

Children find a lot of things terrifying. As adults, our response varies according to whether we judge their fear to be appropriate or not. Where it is appropriate, to our grown-up eyes – fear of a growling dog in the street, for instance – we are still likely to find the child's response at fault in some way. In the case of the dog, we would probably try to slip past at a respectful distance; but the child would be just as likely to scream its head off or grow roots into the pavement. My point is that the child's fear then becomes a problem for the adult to deal with. Even when the child suffers from night terrors, to which most adults tend to respond with sympathy – at least at first – we say things like 'There, there, there's nothing to be afraid of.' This may comfort us, but what does it really say to the child?

When we feel that the fear is inappropriate, it becomes harder still for us simply to be with it, to let it be. All of our own conditioning gets in the way. Were your fears always met with sympathy and respect? Or were you sometimes made to feel ashamed, laughed at or even punished?

The result of all this is that we collect a lot of confused, and confusing, messages about fear. We learn, essentially, not to trust our own responses. We learn to censor them, water them down. In particular, we learn that to scream and 'make a fuss' is more of a nuisance to our parents than to go quiet and withdraw. In other words, a passive fear response is more acceptable than an active one.

In the ordinary way, you sort out enough of these confusions as you grow to emerge as a fully socialised adult. Your original fear responses are acceptably muted, and you carry a lot of unspoken anxieties because you are too afraid to share them, but you get by. Most of us operate on this sort of level. In order to see more clearly how crippling the effects of unexpressed fear can be, we need to look at a more extreme example.

Elaine was thirty-five when she first came into therapy. Her marriage had broken down, and the present crisis was bringing some long-buried feelings to the surface. In addition, her three-year-old daughter was the same age as she had been when – she suspected, but did not yet remember – she had been abused by her father. All the pieces of the puzzle were assembled; it only remained for her to give herself permission to fit them together. For her, therapy was a safe haven where she could at last begin to see her life in its proper perspective.

According to her mother, Elaine had been a lively and precocious toddler. Somewhere between the ages of two and three she had changed, becoming quiet and withdrawn. Elaine herself could not remember a time when she had not lived in 'a haze of fear', and her appearance reflected this; she was very thin, with long hair that shadowed her face, and thick glasses. Her voice was low and monotonous, and her clothes drab and concealing. As a child, she had been bullied by other children, who sensed her fear and were quick to take advantage of it. She was afraid of her parents, her teachers and her peers, and suffered from constant nightmares in which she was always pursued by some terrible monster. Socially and physically inept, her one solace was in reading – she escaped into books or into her own intricate fantasy world.

Elaine had never questioned why she was so different from other children. To a child, things simply are as they are. It was not until she began her therapeutic journey that she began to see what a barren desert her childhood had been, and that there must have been some reason for all those terrors. Slowly, she began to explore, feeling her way through the obscuring haze, back to where it was thickest, where the strongest demons waited.

What Elaine found there, when she finally took her courage in both hands and went voluntarily into that place, was the memory of being sexually abused and almost frightened to death by her father. The memory was the first thing to emerge; the feelings that went with it, the raw terror, the helpless outrage and the sexual shame, did not come through until some time later, by gradual stages. However, as she allowed herself to feel these feelings and own them at last, she went through an astonishing transformation.

The first change was an immediate and dramatic increase in her sexual energy, which had always been fairly low. Elaine had never been able to get properly angry before, had hardly even raised her voice; now, she learned how to shout and scream, and to stand up for herself. She discovered that the more people saw of her, the more they liked what they saw; so she began to take risks, dressing more attractively (which had seemed an incredibly dangerous thing to do) and expressing herself more openly. It had always been too dangerous for her to know her own feelings, let alone show them, and this had been a major cause of the failure of her marriage. Now, at last, she began to be capable of real relationships. In her own words, 'I feel as though I've lived most of my life in black and white, and now, suddenly, the world is full of colour.'

Fear is a paralysing force. In order to survive, Elaine had frozen, cut herself off almost as completely as she could while still living. The price she paid was enormous. Unexpressed and unacknowledged fear leaks out wherever it can, destroying our ability to act and react freely. When it comes to relationships, we are unable to flow, to be spontaneous; there is always a shadow, a hesitation.

It is normal and healthy to sometimes be afraid. But if you are often afraid, if it stops you from engaging with the world, or if you suffer from apparently meaningless terrors or panic attacks, remember: the terrors and panics do have a meaning. Fear does not arise without a cause. You do have a choice whether to honour your feelings or to try to suppress them. The quality of your life depends upon the choice you make.

Exercise 13
Facing your fears

If you've been doing these exercises, you've been working on fear indirectly. Each time you take a risk in this way, sharing your private thoughts and emotions with others and being heard, you push back the frontiers of safety a little further. But a lot of our fears stem from childhood, and if the child inside you feels pushed too far, he or she will find a way to sabotage your progress. So this is an exercise to look after your childish self.

STEP 1

Be in your chosen place, with your partner or chosen companions (not more than three people for this exercise). When it is your turn, take a moment to imagine yourself as a child. Think back to a time when you were afraid. Don't choose something really big to focus on, like physical or sexual abuse; it may be too much for your friends to handle. Were you ever lost, or bullied, or had to do something you were scared of doing? Maybe you were frightened at night with the light off, or maybe you were terrified of the dentist.

Describe the scene to your partner. Talk about yourself as 'I'; speak as though you were back in that time. When you have finished speaking, close your eyes. Take a deep breath and be silent for a moment.

STEP 2

Now imagine that instead of being alone with your fear, you have a wonderful friend or friends, wise and strong and resourceful, who are here to help and protect you. They are here to look after you, and will do whatever you ask.

STEP 3

Open your eyes. Look at your partner. You don't have to be alone and frightened any more. Let that sink in – you are loved. Ask them for whatever you would like. Maybe you'd like just to be held, or maybe you'd like a massage. Perhaps you feel like dancing, playing loud music and making a noise. Perhaps you'd like them to make you something to eat. Whatever it is, give yourself about fifteen minutes to enjoy being looked after.

STEP 4

When everyone has taken their turn, finish the exercise with a quick round – about two minutes each – to say how that felt for you, and to thank your partner or friends. You may feel quite vulnerable afterwards, so make sure you don't have to go straight on to something else.

Anger: the red tide

Childhood rage is definitely a problem for adults to cope with. It is noisy, chaotic and potentially damaging to the child and to any people or things within reach. Moreover, the first rages usually arise when the child's wishes come into conflict with those of the parent, so that the parent has to find some way to deal with them without losing control. The child learns, fairly early on, that losing its temper rarely brings about any positive results, and that disapproval and dismay are probably the mildest reactions it can expect. Later in childhood the reactions get stronger; a child of ten who has a tantrum is likely either to be laughed at or punished.

Our anger, therefore, is another thing that we learn to be ashamed of. If we manage to suppress it, we grow up avoiding conflict as much as we can. When someone at work annoys you, do you find a way to tell them, or do you hold your tongue? If you do not tell them, do you tell other people in your workplace about it, or do you take it home to offload on to your partner? If you do not talk about it at all, what happens to your irritation? Try as you will, you cannot simply make it disappear.

It will go underground, and it will affect you physically, tensing muscles, inhibiting your breathing and hindering the free flow of energy. It will track sideways under the ground and leak out wherever it can find a weak spot, usually when you are dealing with people of whom you are not afraid, such as your children or your partner – your nearest and dearest. The anger will spill out clumsily, inappropriately, wounding those whom you love.

Is it not worth trying to learn a better way to cope with anger? It is such a potent force, a fierce expression of life energy. This is the energy that moves outwards, that gets things done, that engages with the world. In many ways, anger and fear can be seen as opposite, or complementary, forces. Some people say that in order to live peacefully together, we must learn to renounce our anger. They have not understood that if we could really do that, rather than simply suppressing anger, we would also lose our ability to create, to do and to make and to mend. A person who cannot be angry is depressed.

Rather than trying to renounce anger you have to learn how to embrace it. As with fear, if you become familiar and friendly with your anger, you can come through to a place where it becomes an ally. Instead of being overwhelmed by your rage, you can ride it, and use it constructively rather than for destroying. There are no shortcuts; you can't just decide to do this. First, you must learn to express your anger, and honour it as it arises. Next, you have to learn how to modify that expression, to be aware of the effects it has on other people. At the same time as you welcome home your own anger, so you become more comfortable with anger in others, more able to give them permission to express their anger, and less threatened when it is directed at you. Only then can you move on to the third stage, where you gain the power to use it as you wish.

STAGE ONE: LETTING IT LOOSE

Quite often, we do not even know when we are angry. A common way to avoid feeling anger is to sidestep into something else, something more acceptable. For instance, I have a client whose husband is dying of cancer. In our first two sessions, the main emotion that she expressed was a sort of wise sadness. She said that she meditated a lot, and that she had good friends to whom she could talk about anything, and I was left feeling that somehow we had not really met.

In the third session, as we talked about how her husband was struggling with his feelings, I remarked that it must be very hard for her to be sympathetic all the time. Tears sprang to her eyes; she began to sob, and then burst out with 'He's such a bastard to live with!' Immediately she tried to apologise, but this was a moment of truth, and in that moment she came alive. Her eyes brightened, her back straightened and we made real contact for the first time. Her anger was not the whole truth, nor did it cancel out all her other feelings, but her shame and denial had given it more weight than it deserved, and so added to her burdens.

Another way to sidestep is to retreat into the head, and take up the moral high ground of apparent reason and logic. It is infuriating trying to argue with someone who does this. While they remain cool, calm and puzzled by other people's inability to control themselves, everyone else is acting out their unexpressed rage for them.

I remember working in a group with Jonathan, a young man whose family, he said, never touched each other and never showed emotion. In the group, he would offer judgments to others based on how he thought they should behave, and he was bewildered by their hostile reactions. We looked at what had happened the last time he visited his parents, not having seen them for nearly a year. In passing, he mentioned that his father, after a brief greeting, had gone off fishing for the whole weekend. When someone asked if he was not hurt by this, he replied, 'Well, his fishing is very important to him.' There was a sort of collective hiss at this. Surely he minded, even just a little bit, that his father hadn't cared enough to spend ten minutes in his company?

Jonathan continued to deny that he felt anything about it, while all around him people were getting more and more agitated. In the end another young man, Adam, jumped up and asked if he could 'speak for' Jonathan to his father. Jonathan shrugged and said that was fine by him. Addressing a cushion as the father, Adam said 'Hi, Dad! Anybody in there? Hey, I'd like to talk to you. It really hurt when you went off like that. You hardly waited to say hello to me. Aren't I worth even five minutes of your attention?'

As he watched, Jonathan's face twisted in pain. He looked at his 'father' and said, 'Yes, it does hurt. You couldn't even be bothered to be there. Fishing was more important than your son. Pretty well everything is more important.' Suddenly he was sobbing, difficult, tearing sobs, shaking with the force of the grief flowing through him. With the grief came rage, all the helpless anger of a child not listened to, not interesting enough to be bothered with. It poured out of him incoherently, messily, and it was far easier to be with than his usual detachment had been, because it was real, and strong and alive. Typically, Jonathan was afraid afterwards that he might have 'upset' people. Instead, he found that their anger had gone completely. Expecting to be 'told off', he found himself congratulated.

In this first stage, when you are finding your way back into feelings that have been long suppressed or barely held in check, you can't be graceful in the way you express them. They just need to blast their way out. Your task is not to try to control them any more, but to find safe places where you can give yourself permission to let go.

This often means a therapeutic setting, whether in a group or one to one, with a facilitator who understands how to prepare the way and can help to integrate the changes that will happen. However, it can also mean a strong relationship, where there is enough trust and commitment and wisdom to contain the blast. Once you go beyond the first stage of relationship, these feelings tend to arise of their own accord in any case, as the wounded spirit tries to heal itself. It's up to you whether you try to push them down, dump them onto your partner or form the intention to work through them.

Exercise 14
Dealing with anger

The shape of this exercise depends on how you handle feelings within your relationship – or with your friends, if you do not have a partner. Do you lose your temper easily, or do you bottle up your anger and go cold, refusing to talk? Does one of you shout and the other try to stay calm, or do you get into full-blown screaming matches?

FOR THOSE WHO TEND TO HIDE THEIR ANGER

If you are someone who normally tries to hide your anger, try the exercise this way. Maybe you don't even know you're angry about something until hours or even days later. So this is an exercise about bringing out your anger in a safe way.

STEP 1

Get together in the usual way; sometime in the evening is best, so that you can review the day that's just gone by. When you speak, take the time to see if anything annoyed you today. It doesn't matter how trivial it was – in fact it's easier to practice on small things at first. Were you ignored in a shop as you waited to be served? Did you have to make too many phone calls to sort something out? Did someone at work upset you? For now, leave aside your anger with the person you're speaking to (if you have any); you want them to be your ally in this exercise. Allow yourself to notice how it feels to be taken for granted, given poor service or short-changed in some way.

In this space, it is safe to express your feelings, even to exaggerate them a little. In the next chapter we will be looking at how to manage conflicts in your close relationships, but for now this is a first step in bringing out your feelings and being heard.

STEP 2

As the listener, your job is to show your response without words. As your partner describes things that have happened, you may feel angry yourself, but stay with it; this is not your turn to speak. Be supportive; if your partner is having trouble finding their feelings, just give them the space. Afterwards, thank them; even if they said very little, it is a step in the right direction.

FOR THOSE WHO TEND TO FLY OFF THE HANDLE

Now for the second version of the exercise. If you are someone who normally flies off the handle very easily, practise holding back. When you feel yourself getting angry, breathe deeply and say nothing; turn away from whoever is provoking you if necessary. Again, try this in trivial situations at first, where it does not matter too much. If you get a phone call trying to sell you double glazing, do you normally shout? Try a quiet 'No thank you' and put the phone down. Do you go in for road rage? Put the radio on and focus on that instead. Tell yourself that you have the space, later, to let off steam.

STEP 1

When you speak, recall the incidents that made you angry and describe how you felt at the time. Give yourself full permission to be as angry as you like. Talk about what you did instead of shouting at the time, and how it feels now to have done that. The chances are that you won't feel so annoyed any more; the moment has passed. Notice how you feel about yourself if you didn't shout. Do you feel pleased with yourself? Do you feel more powerful? Give yourself some appreciation; this is a difficult lesson to learn.

STEP 2

This time, the second person will give feedback after listening. Don't offer advice or suggestions on what your partner did, or could have done. Just give your appreciation of the effort they made. Angry people are used to getting reactions from those around them; it's part of the payoff.

Not getting those reactions may be just as strange as not showing your anger, and you need lots of positive reinforcement to make up for all the negative attention you won't be getting. Little by little you will be able to modify your anger reflex, and that energy will become available to you to use constructively, instead of wasting it and getting yourself disliked.

STAGE TWO: RIDING THE RAPIDS

When you no longer have trouble giving free rein to your anger, then – and only then – can you begin to modify the way in which you express it. You must first learn to honour your own feelings, before you can truly be responsive to the feelings of others. In the second stage, you have to learn to take responsibility for yourself, and to recognise that what you do with your feelings has a profound effect on those around you.

This is true of all feelings, but it is probably most obvious with anger. When you shout, people notice. You may be shouting at no one, or at one person in particular, but everyone within hearing will be affected in some way. Some people – those who are most comfortable with their own anger – can handle it without being rocked too badly, but most will be upset in some way, and will react with fear, distress or anger in turn. It is almost impossible to remain indifferent.

You therefore have to recognise, from a place of maturity and inner knowing that is very different from the sanctions imposed upon you as a child, that you do not have the right to invade other people with your anger. Once the first urgency of self-expression is past, you must learn to choose the right times and places to voice your anger. You must also learn to modify it according to the recipient, if there is one. Some people are more easily wounded than others. Children are the obvious example, but all of us are more vulnerable at some times than at others. If you push too hard with your anger, you simply push people into putting up their defences, and then communication is lost.

Renata was a client of mine who worked in a residential care community. Her work meant that she had to be in close and continuous contact with her colleagues. She had a history of abuse and other deeply wounding experiences as a child, but rather than trying to bury her anger, Renata was constantly living it. She would fly into a rage when she did not get her own way, and whatever other people gave her was never enough. After a time people simply avoided her whenever they could, with the result that she became very isolated. This was a familiar place for her, and she was miserable in it, but she could not see the way out.

The whole community came to be dominated by Renata and her tantrums, until one person finally dared to risk challenging her, and to point out in as loving a way as possible that she was overwhelming everyone with her anger and driving them away. Somehow, the fact that he had cared enough to do this, at the risk of inciting her wrath, got through to her, and she was grateful.

Renata went into therapy to begin the task of tracing her feelings to their source. Slowly, over a period of many years, she learned that she did not have to be angry to feel real, and she learned to express her anger without vomiting it over other people. It can be a long, hard journey, but becoming mindful of others is the other side of honouring your own feelings. For relationships to be possible, the two must go hand in hand.

STAGE THREE: LEARNING TO MASTER ANGER

Anger is a rising emotion. If you have time to notice, you can feel how it moves up through your body from the depths of your belly to your head. It demands to be released through action of some sort. If you have learned not to let it overwhelm you completely, it is possible to focus on this rising energy, allowing it to well up inside you and fill your whole being while you stay calm and in control. Sometimes this is described as 'cold rage', and you might have experienced it in a situation where you feel angry but also powerful; seeing a bigger child bullying a smaller one, perhaps. If you can contain the charge and stay with it, a transformation happens. It no longer feels like anger that you are holding, but pure, intense life force.

If you can harness your anger in this way, it becomes a tremendous source of power and creativity, for anger is nothing more than vital energy rising in response to blockage or frustration of some sort. Before you can do this whenever you want to, you first have to be easy with the full and uncontrolled expression of your anger, and you do have to be able to hold it back as well.

As I said at the beginning of this section, there are no shortcuts. It comes with long and hard experience. Two people come to mind, whom I believe to be masters of this art. One is Nelson Mandela, and the other is the Dalai Lama. Both have every right to be enraged, not just over wrongs done to them personally, but also over the horrors suffered by their people. However, they do not fulminate against their enemies, or incite violence and retribution. Instead, they use that energy, that passion, to inspire others and to create, rather than destroying. If they can choose to do this, so can you.

Grief: the cleansing river

There is an image that sticks in my mind as a potent illustration of the way our society handles grief. After a plane crash in which a lot of people were killed, one newspaper carried the photograph of a child, a boy of about eight or nine, standing by the newly dug grave of his mother and father. The article that went with it praised him for his courage, because as he watched the burial of his parents he had shed no tears.

What kind of courage is this? What kind of madness is it that does not allow a child to howl and scream and rage at the loss of his own parents? It is regarded as perfectly normal, in fact, not to take children to funerals at all – presumably in case it upsets them. It is also normal for people, especially women, to take tranquillisers when they are bereaved, to help deaden the pain. Here is one place where our feelings can be so intense that it can feel as though we, too, will die if we don't express them, yet still we do our utmost to keep them down.

Of course, a moderate display of grief is allowed, at least in the first few days following a major bereavement. It is quite acceptable for women, though less so for men, to cry at funerals. After a week or so, however, people no longer want to hear about it. They are embarrassed, and they try to talk about something more cheerful, or they avoid you altogether.

When it comes to the kind of loss that ranks lower on the scale, there is even less tolerance or understanding. Grief is a natural human response to any kind of loss, whether it be the loss of a loved one through death or departure, the loss of a job, leaving one home for another or the loss of health or hopes. Then there are the hidden losses that are hardly even acknowledged, the miscarriages and stillbirths and abortions, the endings of secret affairs; the loss of freedom and independence that comes to a woman when, however joyfully, she becomes a mother; or the gradual, continual loss of youth and dreams and opportunities, as you choose one path rather than another.

What happens to this great weight of unexpressed grief? Does it work to distract yourself with other things or to smother the grief with drugs? I am reminded of a client who was referred to me because for the last few months, for no apparent physical reason, he had lost all interest in sex. When we met, he told me that this started when his mistress of many years finally ended their affair because he would not leave his wife. 'At first, I was depressed', he said, 'But now I don't feel anything.' What he really meant was that at first he had been feeling his pain, but now he had shut down his feelings and his sex drive had gone with them. This is depression; and this is what happens when you deny yourself the right to grieve. I can illustrate the process best with another example.

Serena came to therapy in her early fifties. She was an elegant, very composed woman, but in the last few years had become increasingly disabled by panic attacks and fits of crying. She could not tolerate being in crowds, and was unable to cope with conflicts, even minor ones. She said that she had been depressed for many years.

There were two obvious major traumas in her life. When she was in her early twenties and still living with her parents, her sister was killed in a car accident. The shock paralysed the entire family; a wall of unexpressed grief went up, and what had been a happy and vibrant family environment became sterile. Serena herself had been a carefree and fun-loving girl; now, she became much more serious and introverted.

A few years later, she met and married Daniel, and with her marriage she rediscovered her joy in living. For ten years, they were very happy together. The marriage was brought to an abrupt end when Daniel discovered that he had a particularly virulent form of cancer, from which, after only three months of illness, he died. Serena 'coped', because she felt she had to, but what she did not do was to cope with her own agony. It was simply too much for her, and there were other people to look after, and things that had to be done – as there usually are. So she discounted her feelings, found ways of distracting herself. She took up social work in an area where she was constantly dealing with grief and pain in her clients; but it did not help her to discharge her own pain.

Slowly, over many months, we began to explore her grief. My job was to provide the environment in which she could do this, an environment that simply was not available to her in her everyday life. Serena herself, witnessed and supported by me, allowed herself to re-experience the deaths of her husband and her sister. She opened up the places that she had not gone into at the time, feeling what was there to be felt, and expressing what was crying out for expression. Week after week, she would spend whole sessions sobbing.

Sometimes it seemed that there was no end to her tears, that her fears were justified and that once she had begun, she would never stop crying. Often, she would be torn between the need for release and the urge to close down, to feel no more pain. What kept her going was her own deeper wisdom; the sense that she was keeping faith with herself and with her own dead loved ones. Little by little, as Serena restored her grief to its rightful place, it stopped leaking into other parts of her life. The panic attacks, the weeping for no apparent reason, and the mental confusion and fear of crowds all dropped away. So, gradually, did her sense of depression. She began to come alive again.

At the same time, healing was taking place. Over the months, Serena's traumatic losses began to lose their paralysing power over her. She could remember the lives of her husband and her sister, as well as their deaths. Huge areas of her own life that had become taboo because of their painful associations now opened up to her again. Serena no longer sees it as a weakness to need therapy, for she is far stronger now than she ever was before. Three years on, she is training to be a counsellor herself, and she will be a wise and compassionate one. Unafraid of her own depths, she will be able to be with her clients as they go into and through theirs.

You cannot possibly grieve too much. The body knows, and the spirit knows, when enough is enough. Our minds are not equipped to judge these things. Nor can you possibly make too much noise about it, whatever other people may think. In many other cultures, and particularly in less sophisticated ones than our own, it is part of the ritual of mourning to wail and to scream, to tear your clothes or even your own flesh in the intensity of grief. In the act of weeping – not just a few discreet tears, but the deep, loud, wrenching sobbing that can go on for hours – we shed more than we realise. There is a kind of ecstasy in grief, a loss of self that happens when we allow ourselves to go deeply into our pain without holding back. In that place, there is healing.

The process of grieving after a major loss takes about two years to go through if you allow it to happen without blocking. For the first six months the grief is intense, and dominates your life. Over the next eighteen months or so, healing and recovery will happen. However, if you do block the process, or distract yourself – with work, new relationships, alcohol or drugs, and so on – recovery may never happen. You can carry your griefs for a lifetime, and a lifetime of grief is what you will have.

Exercise 15
Honouring your grief

You can't grieve to order. Your grief can't really be set aside to be brought out later in your five-minute exercise at the end of the day. There are many techniques for dealing with grief – both old and new – in therapy, but within your partnership, you can make one very simple agreement. When either of you feels sad about something, make a pact that you will ask for some support from the other. The kind of support that is needed is not comforting words, sympathy or bracing advice. All you need is holding. Physical holding is best of all, but a listening ear on the phone is better than nothing.

When you give yourself permission to ask for support in this way and your partner gives you permission to express what you are feeling, with words or tears or whatever it may be, you will find that it is not such a big deal. Unless your grief is new and overwhelming, you are not going to sob for hours and hours. A few minutes, at most, is all you will need; then thank your partner, and move on. In this way, you can build in the space for grief and sadness without it overshadowing every-thing else in your life. In fact, you will find that there is more space for joy and laughter as well.

There is a beauty about someone who is truly grieving that is very different from the dull, heavy feeling of someone who is depressed. Once you are comfortable with your own capacity for mourning, it is not hard to keep company with those who have been bereaved. It can be deeply moving, even inspiring. What is difficult and uncomfortable is to be with someone who will not allow themselves to feel their own grief. It is there, unexpressed and unacknowledged, and it casts a pall over everything.

The implications for relationships are clear. To hold back grief is to dull the edge of feeling, and so to diminish the possibility of intimacy. To allow it, on the other hand, is to offer your partner a great gift. If he or she is able to accept it, both partners will be richer. If you can grieve together, then you can also rejoice together.

Coming home to the heartland

Does it look like a lot of hard work? Well, it is and it isn't. At first, there may be quite an emotional backlog to clear, but once you and your partner get better at expressing yourselves to each other and more confident that you will be heard, it will get much easier. Then you can deal with things as they come up. Recognising and honouring your own feelings, and those of your partner, becomes one of the many threads that are woven into your relationship, rather than a minefield where one false step could blow it all apart.

We've looked at how you can set about the task of learning to express your feelings freely and honestly, and how you can help your partner do so as well. The feelings that tend to get 'stuck' are those of fear, anger and grief, and we've looked at ways to begin to free them up. In the next chapter, we take a close look at the conflicts that can arise in relationships, and how to handle them.

Chapter 6
Conflict Management – Riding the Storms

As long as we are on earth, the love that unites us will bring us suffering by our very contact with one another, because this love is the resetting of a body of broken bones. Even saints cannot live with saints on this earth without some anguish, without some pain at the differences that come between them.

Thomas Merton, American monk,
writer and poet, 1915–1968

Conflict is an essential and healthy part of relationship. If we are to express ourselves and our needs at all, we will have conflict. Intentionally or unintentionally, we hurt each other just in the course of day-to-day living, as is illustrated by the following case study.

Martin and Kim came to see me together. After nearly five years of marriage they were about to split up. They were very polite to each other, very considerate, and I noticed that when they talked about their troubles it was always with a smile.

We began to explore the history of their relationship. It was sexual magnetism that had drawn them together, and the dreams that they shared – to travel the world, to have children. For about six months, they were in bliss. Then Kim became pregnant. She was delighted, but for Martin it brought up a lot of fear. He was afraid that their magical relationship would be weighed down by responsibilities, and he also thought that he had to let go of the idea of travelling.

He could not share wholeheartedly in Kim's joy, but instead of talking about his fears, he withdrew emotionally, not wanting to upset her. Kim, of course, was both upset and angry at his withdrawal, which she did not understand; but she also tried to hold back her anger. Martin, sensing it in a thousand subtle ways, withdrew further. Into this troubled atmosphere their first child was born.

Their son was three years old by the time they came for counselling, and the gulf between them had grown so wide that they no longer felt there was a relationship to work on. Amicable separation was what they hoped to achieve. Nevertheless, as we worked together, it became plain that there was a great deal of unexpressed hurt between them. When I invited them to speak some of their feelings to each other, Martin was very nervous and afraid. Kim, on the other hand, was excited at the opportunity to express her anger, and she felt that the therapeutic setting gave her the permission and the safety to do so.

As Kim opened up her store of long-held resentment, the automatic smiles disappeared. Martin's own resentment came to the surface, and he spoke about his fear and rage as he saw his dreams dwindling away. In the weeks that followed, they began to learn how to express their feelings and to listen to each other. As they struggled to share their truths without tearing at each other, so an unexpected enjoyment of these spirited encounters began to grow. What had been a dry and arid relationship became a juicy one. Through the spark of conflict, the spark of love was rekindled.

Conventional wisdom says that relationships are destroyed by the wounds that we inflict upon each other through what we say and do, but my observation is that the reverse is true: far more relationships break up over what is *not* said, than over what *is* said. Today, Martin and Kim have a marriage that works. They are struggling with the issues of freedom and commitment – and a host of other things – but they have both learned to bring their honesty and passion into their everyday relating.

What can we do about conflict? In order to bring the art of conflict into its rightful place in relationships, we have to confront in ourselves the deep-rooted conviction that conflict is wrong. Quarrelling is a sign that something is amiss. If I were a better human being, or if you were less controlling, selfish, bad-tempered, we wouldn't need to fight. In a perfect relationship there is perfect harmony. Maybe I'm with the wrong person . . .

All of this is rubbish, and it serves you not at all when it comes to making strong, resilient, loving relationships. In trying to sweep things under the carpet or treating them as a major disaster when an argument happens, you lose a precious opportunity to learn a little more about each other, to become more intimate. Just as you discover when you begin to honour your own feelings, there is much more to the territory of conflict than you can possibly imagine from the sort of hit-and-run skirmishes around its edges that are the usual stuff of fights between partners. Here, too, there is tremendous potential for transformation, if you can only summon up the courage to stay with feelings and situations that are painful for you.

Learning the language

Once again, it is a question of learning the language; of listening to yourself and to your partner, and noticing what you do when a clash happens. You can't stop to analyse what is going on when you are in the middle of it, but you can make an agreement to do so afterwards, and to discuss it with others outside the partnership as well. The simple act of making an agreement like this – preferably not in the heat of the moment, but when both partners are cold sober – immediately begins to transform the way you approach conflict and the way you handle it.

What is the language of conflict? At the simplest level, it arises when one partner tries to express feelings to the other and is met with either hurt or anger, or both. Defences then come into play, and you will notice that you have favourite ways of reacting. All the many forms of defence can be put into two groups: those that involve withdrawal, and those that involve attack. Withdrawal means closing down, retiring hurt, refusing to talk any more, or – more subtly – trying to move the ground of the conflict, and arguing from your head or shaming your partner for getting into a state. Attack means trying to wound, bringing up old scores, shouting, physically assaulting. There are, of course, infinite variations on these two themes.

Typically, an argument involves a confused and confusing mixture of tactics, with both combatants frequently shifting ground and trying to gain an advantage. It ends with the withdrawal or collapse of one partner, but both usually go away feeling wounded and morally superior. You may attempt reconciliation, but you tend to skimp on inspecting the wounds too closely in case you stir up further conflict. You try to smooth over the hurt, to forgive and let go and get back to 'normal', and the original hurt is now overlaid with new hurts got in the heat of the battle. It is no wonder that conventional wisdom regards conflict as inherently bad and destructive, for unless you can learn some better ways of handling it, it cannot be anything else.

How can you make conflict constructive? This chapter deals with some of the ways in which you can begin to work with it, and it also looks at the art of forgiveness, or the healing of old wounds. I want to emphasise, however, that this is no easy undertaking. It is hard and painful work, and although you gain experience along the way, it will never be effortless, never without pain. It is the effort itself, choosing to go through the agony again and yet again, that gives birth to love, and provides it with the nourishment that it needs to grow.

Exercise 16
Learning your own language

STEP 1

Meet in the usual way with your partner or one close friend. You are going to focus on an argument or a heated encounter that has happened in the last few days, with someone not present at this moment. For now, you are working on understanding your own part in the conflict, not on trying to resolve it with the other person. So it could be to do with your partner (if they are not present), a friend, someone at work or perhaps a family member.

Describe the argument to your listening partner in the present tense, as if it were happening now. Then go back to the beginning and describe it again, but rather than simply telling the story, focus on how you are feeling. At each stage, pause and ask yourself what is going on inside you. If you are angry, what do you do to deal with the anger? If you are feeling guilty or defensive or ashamed, how do you deal with that? In this exercise, the listener can give you some verbal help as you go along. For example, they might say, 'Hang on a minute. Say some more about what was going on for you just then', or 'You say you felt hurt by what she said. Are you sure that's all you felt?'

The point is that in the heat of the moment, we tend to go into emergency alert mode, and a lot of our responses are unconscious. How often have you walked away and only later thought of the perfect riposte? Or, when your blood has cooled, looked back in horror at what you said or did? The more you can become conscious of what you do when you feel under attack, the more choice you have about how to do it differently. Once again, it comes down to noticing and then making choices.

STEP 2

Your partner or friend now takes their turn. You listen, drawing them out if they need it. Notice as you listen where you would have reacted differently. Notice where your feelings differ from those of your partner. While you are listening in this way, the message will be filtering through that there are many possible ways to handle these difficult situations. You are beginning to pick up ideas about how to do it differently.

STEP 3

Talk about what each of you has observed. Stick mostly to what you notice about your own responses, but if you have been impressed by the way your friend or partner handled something, say so. Think about what you would like to do differently, and look at possible ways to change your behaviour. At this stage, this is enough; forming intentions can come later. Thank each other, and finish the exercise.

Setting the stage

1. COMMITMENT

I have talked about making an agreement that, when clashes happen, time will be set aside to look at what is going on. This means that both partners must be willing to explore their own dark places, and to work towards change. In other words, this is the point at which the issue of commitment arises.

Unless both partners are willing to grow with and through the areas where they run into trouble, the relationship will inevitably move towards compromise, stagnation or death. If they are willing, however, it is immensely helpful to make some conscious statement of commitment. This does not have to be 'till death us do part', but it does mean declaring an intention to stay with the process as it unfolds, not to cut and run when things get difficult.

This is an essential step towards establishing trust and making it safe within the relationship for whatever needs to emerge. Just as becoming a parent means – in theory at least – making a pledge to be there for the new human being until he can be there for himself, so entering into mature relationships involves the same sort of commitment.

Having said that, I want to emphasise that unless *both* partners are willing to commit themselves to growing and working with what comes up, there can be no deal. If you are living with someone who is abusive, physically or emotionally, and they are not willing to change, then you owe it to yourself to get out. There is no merit in allowing yourself to be abused, and no benefit for either partner if you stay. Unless each of you can give honour and respect to the other, the relationship cannot evolve.

Most of us find the idea of commitment a little frightening, and for many it is terrifying. We fear being trapped, shackled to someone who may turn out to be a nightmare to live with; and what if someone better comes along? I have seen so many relationships that have been on the brink of moving into a new and more mature phase come to grief because one partner or the other could not bring themselves to commit.

However, it need not be like that. Some years ago, a friend of mine, Michael, was considering training to be an osteopath. The course was four years long and full time, and Michael had no prospect of financial help. The reaction of many people he knew was, 'How can you possibly make that kind of commitment? Who knows where you'll be in four years' time?' Michael said that if he looked at it that way, the thought of those four years filled him with dread. However, he had been drifting for some years now, not realising any of his dreams, and if he did not jump one way or another he could still be doing that for the next four years.

The only way to make it possible was to make the commitment, day by day and week by week, to be with what he was doing right now. He took the course and finished it, and is now a successful practitioner. Along the way, his closest friends became those who were also willing to take the risk of throwing their energy into making their dreams come true.

It is the same when you make a heart commitment. All you can do is to pledge yourself, as fully as you can, for this moment. However, in the making of a pledge like this, magic happens. When you really throw your energy into a relationship – with the conscious knowledge that it will always be less than 100 per cent, simply because you are human – you create momentum.

You create a place where the relationship can expand and you can be open to the adventure and the wonder of it, as well as to the burdens. If you give it as much as you can today, you are more than likely still to be here tomorrow, and next week; and it will not be the same. You will be moving, and growing.

What are you committing yourself to? Simply this: to keep company with each other on your journey of self-realisation. As trust grows, and love grows, and you learn to express what you are feeling, so your patterns and issues from the past will surface, seeking resolution. Unconsciously at first, you will play them out within the partnership. Conflict will arise, and in that conflict is the key to becoming conscious, owning what works for you, discarding what doesn't and healing old wounds.

These things will begin to happen whether you commit yourself or not, but if you do not commit, there will be no container in which to hold them, and the relationship is likely to founder. Once the commitment is in place, you can begin to look at some other ways of containing conflict, so that rather than simply suffering it, you can begin to use it.

2. CLEAR INTENTIONS

With commitment and the resolution to use your differences creatively goes the forming of clear ideas about where you want your conflicts to take you. Again, this cannot be done at the height of the battle, but at some more peaceful time, preferably when neither partner is actively feeling hurt.

What it comes down to is the conscious intention to reach an outcome in which no one is the loser. If you are determined to win at all costs, your relationship is doomed. Creative conflict is not about wounding, scoring points, getting revenge or emerging victorious. It is about reaching a 'win–win situation', a place where both partners feel heard and respected, even if they do not necessarily get what they were originally fighting for.

It means shifting the focus from whatever the fight was apparently about – which is often just a hook for all kinds of other things in any case – to the quality of the interaction that goes on before, during and after the engagement. It means getting better at listening, and at expressing your feelings so that you can be heard. At the root of conflict is hurt, on one side or on both, and if this can be honoured through expression by one person and acknowledgment by the other, the charge will be defused. It is easy to tell when this has happened, because the energy goes out of the fight, and softer feelings come to the fore.

In a relationship, the desire to attack or to wound another person always springs from your own pain. You may succeed in wounding them, but although that makes you feel strong, your pain remains unheard and you have created an enemy. This is often at its most obvious in divorce proceedings, in which two people who once loved each other go all out to humiliate and blame and score all the points they can, while nursing their hurt and grief in private. Who – apart from the lawyers – really benefits from this? And who, in their heart of hearts, really wants it?

Forming the intention that both partners should emerge as winners brings about a radical shift in the dynamics of conflict management. The intention will not automatically become the reality, but it is a step towards it. As the proverb says, 'To travel hopefully is better than to arrive'.

Exercise 17
How to avoid conflict

Part of conflict management is about prevention. In other words, this means looking at how and where problems arise and trying to change the situation so that you don't get into the conflict in the first place.

Some conflicts are unavoidable. A great many, however – especially in relationships – are sparked by scarcity; one or other (or both) of you is feeling they are not getting enough of something. It could be love, time, sex or attention. Whatever it is, there is not enough to go around. And it's too easy, in partnership, to blame or resent your partner when you are not getting enough. So this is an exercise in lateral thinking, to try to meet some of those demands

without loading them onto your partner. You can do this one together with one or more people, or on your own.

STEP 1

Take a piece of paper and divide it into two columns. The first is headed 'Giving out', and the second 'Taking in'. In the first column, list the things you do that involve giving out energy. This might include work, looking after children or elderly relatives, housework, and so forth. Obviously, some of these things are rewarding as well as demanding, but the point here is that they tend to draw on your resources.

STEP 2

Now go to the column headed 'Taking in'. Here, you can list all the things you do that nourish you, that leave you refreshed and replenished. This could include all sorts of things, from going for walks – as long as it's not just because you have to walk the dog – to time out with friends, to classes and concerts and visits to the gym. It doesn't include holidays or even weekend breaks, unless you take them very frequently; this is about everyday life.

STEP 3

Look at your two columns. Is there a balance there? Do you feel there is enough nourishment in your life, or do you feel depleted, worn down by it all? Do you build in daily and weekly times to care for yourself, or do you muddle along, hoping that your holiday in three months' time will set you up again? If you are satisfied with the way your life is running, well done! As long as this is not achieved at your partner's expense, you have set yourself up to be available for a relationship that does not involve wrangling over scarce resources.

STEP 4

If you don't feel you are getting enough, think again. Are there things you used to do that have fallen by the wayside? Are there things you'd like to do, or to learn, but have never made the time for? Would you simply like an hour in the day when you can fall asleep if you want to?

Start to look at ways in which you can build in some nourishing time, preferably on a daily basis, but certainly several times a week. Some of this will involve your partner looking after the children, cooking a meal, or whatever, but make sure that most of it can be achieved in other ways. If you have small children, for example, arrange with other parents to mind each other's children on a regular basis, so that the children have some fun together and you get your time off. If you and your partner fall out over cleaning the house, think about getting a cleaner. If it's hard to justify going to a class or an event by yourself, go with a friend. It gets easier with practice!

STEP 5

Keep a diary in which you can record the things you've done that are nourishing for you, and plan in activities yet to come. This is one more way of making sure you stay conscious about what you are doing – or not doing. You will know from your own sense of well-being when you are doing enough. What feeds you will also feed your relationship, and you will find that the areas where conflict can arise will get smaller.

3. THE ART OF TIMING

There are several important points to be made about timing, which can make an immense difference to the way in which you handle conflict. In chapter 5 I talked about learning to express anger and the way in which, once you have learned to express it freely, you have to learn how to modify that expression. This has a direct bearing on the management of conflict, in that you can't begin to do this until you are comfortable with feeling your own feelings, and capable of holding them until the time is right for their expression.

Having said that, the first point to be made about timing is not to leave it too long before saying what you need to say. If you allow things to build past the point where you are able to express them gracefully, there is likely to be an ugly and explosive scene. We have all seen this happen in work situations, where people may hold irritations with each other for a long time, and then suddenly lose control completely over something apparently trivial. To speak out at the time and on the ground of your choosing is empowering; to lose your cool or allow yourself to be goaded into a reaction is not.

The second point follows from the first. Don't hold it too long, but do choose your moment. Remember that in a relationship the most constructive outcome is that both partners 'win', so choose your time carefully. Try to ensure that neither of you is in a hurry to be somewhere else, too tired or carrying other burdens. If other people are around – children, for instance – with whom you do not feel free to say what may need to be said, make sure that your meeting will not be overheard or interrupted.

If you are the challenger, opening a dialogue that you know may bring up feelings of hurt or anger, then you must be generous; you are in the stronger position, and it will not help if you place your partner at a disadvantage. I recently went to dinner with some friends and among the other guests were a barrister and his wife. During the meal, he made several disparaging remarks about his wife's lack of intellect and achievement, clearly looking for support among his friends there. Not only was he perfectly comfortable with sparring in public, but he was also enjoying the fact that his wife was not. She was embarrassed, angry and hurt, but ashamed to show it in company, so she got back at him in various covert ways, which made her appear shrewish and ungracious. Their sniping poisoned the atmosphere and did not improve anyone's digestion. This is something that couples who are in trouble often do, but trying to get support in underhanded ways like this does not achieve anything except more bad feeling.

The third point about time is the understanding that whatever you say or do in the heat of battle should not be given too much weight. Somewhere in the process of healing your self-esteem and attending to your own wounds from the past, you gain the ability to take things lightly. When you are attacked, you can see – sometimes – that the attacker is acting from a place of pain, and you no longer have to fall victim to it. Conversely, if you have hurt someone – whether deliberately or not – you can find the grace and the generosity to apologise or make amends.

In the middle of a red-hot argument, however, this is far beyond your reach – and it is perfectly all right that it should be this way. During a fight, people speak and act from their anger, their hurt, their guilt. You simply need to be mad for a while, to go 'out of your mind' and let it all spill out, clumsy and inarticulate and unreasonable and outrageous as it may be. Children do this beautifully, yelling insults and getting into a killing rage with their siblings or close friends – and parents too, if their parents are wise enough to let them – but they do not hold it against each other for long. Once the storm has passed, they will play peacefully together.

From this you can learn the wisdom of giving it time, of letting things settle after a battle, and not trying to hammer it out endlessly or take each other to task for what you said in anger yesterday. There is a kind of dance in conflict. After an engagement in which strong feelings have been aired, it makes sense to move apart for a time, to take space and allow those feelings to subside. They are not the whole truth, and with time other, more gentle feelings will rise to the surface. It becomes possible to see the other person's point of view, even if you still do not agree with it.

Now is the time to come together again, to acknowledge the hurts that have been given, and to talk over the new thoughts and feelings that have emerged. Sometimes resolution happens without any effort at all, because self-expression was all that was needed. At other times there is a great deal of work to be done, as the conflict uncovers issues that need to be worked on. The main point here is that the argument itself is not the end of the world, although it may feel like it at the time. It is part of a process, and that process will take time to unfold.

4. GETTING SUPPORT

The old way of dealing with disagreements was to avoid them as far as possible, and if that was not possible, to fight in private. In our culture, it is unusual to see people lose their tempers in public. When we do it, we feel that we have 'lost face', unless it is a case of righteous indignation. There is a general disapproval of people who 'air their dirty linen' in front of others, although doing it covertly, like the couple I described earlier, is actually very common.

Hence we often find it very difficult to build a support network that can contain conflict. It is one thing to discuss your grievances with friends who will affirm you and pass judgment on your partner, but this does not actually help the relationship to grow. For that you need friends and counsellors who are willing to act as witnesses – who will reflect back to you their sense of what is going on. You need, at times, to use them as 'seconds', to be present while you try to disentangle the strands of hurt and pain in the relationship. Then you can ask them to hold the boundaries of the engagement, interpret your words to each other, identify the patterns that emerge, and make sure that both sides have been expressed and heard.

In this area of relationships, more than anywhere else, you simply cannot do it on your own. It is one of the great tragedies of our time that, although relationship guidance is freely available through Relate and other forms of counselling, people so often only turn to this resource in desperation, when it is already too late and the relationship has been damaged beyond healing.

The time to call on the support of friends or counsellors is when you feel that things have begun to drift and you cannot address the problem on your own. Perhaps you have tried to express your feelings and have not been met; perhaps you are afraid of what your partner's reaction will be. Get support; bring in a friend or friends, people who care about both of you, and whom you can both trust. Choose the time and the place, and give the issue the energy it deserves. Both the partnership and the friendship will be enriched in the process.

Forgiveness: good housekeeping

When you have been hurt by someone, whether it happened twenty minutes or twenty years ago, a bond is formed. Whether you acknowledge it or not, you invest energy in that person. If you do not or cannot choose to express your hurt feelings, then the bond remains, and it continues to take energy.

As human beings we are constantly striving to be whole, to realise ourselves more fully. So it is that old wounds will ache from time to time, reminding us that healing is not complete. It is the peculiar property of intimate relationships, what makes them such an extraordinary crucible for transformation, that whether we are aware of it or not we will try to use them to settle these old scores.

If, for example, you had a teacher at school who humiliated you in some way, you would have had to swallow your feelings of shame and rage or invite further trouble. These feelings leave a stain, a sensitive place; and when, years later, your partner says or does something that evokes that childhood wound, both of you will be taken aback by the vigour and intensity of your reaction. In fact, you may well unconsciously set this up to happen.

If the whole process remains unconscious, your partner will feel unjustly attacked and you will be left nursing your hurt. This business of 'dumping on' a partner goes on a lot in relationships, and it is a repeated invitation to wake up, start to put your house in order and attend to all those old wounds. As you do start to wake up, as you honour your own feelings and learn the language of the other, it becomes more and more imperative that you undertake this work of forgiveness for both your own sake and that of your loved ones.

Forgiveness, then, is an act of creation; a sweeping out of dark corners and a freeing up of energy that can be put to good use in the here and now. It does not mean turning the other cheek, practising saintliness and being 'nice' to your persecutors. In doing that, you do further violence to yourself. Nor does it mean simply deciding to forget about it and get on with living. Before you can do that, there is a process that you must go through, *and there are no short cuts.* This process is outlined below.

Five steps to forgiveness

1. INTENTION

Once again, it is very important to be clear in your intentions. You cannot forgive because someone else wants you to. The only valid starting point for forgiveness is the point where you have healed your self-esteem enough to know, however dimly, that not forgiving is holding you to your pain. Once, the feelings of anger and hurt, or the desire for retribution, may have helped you to survive, but now you have other and healthier uses for the energy invested there. So your intention is to free yourself for your own benefit. If you still want reparation or revenge, you are not yet ready to forgive.

2. HONOURING THE PAIN

Before you can forgive, you have to honour your own feelings. If you have been wounded, you will feel hurt. Whether you are aware of it or not, you will also be angry. There may be a host of other feelings, too, depending on the circumstances. The task in hand is to allow these feelings without censorship and without trying to water them down. You may need witnesses, you may need help and you will certainly need time. It can be done through therapy, and through a thousand creative projects, involving (for example) writing, painting, acting or making a garden.

You may need to go over the same ground again and again, slowly and patiently, reliving and releasing a little each time. Deep wounds cannot discharge all at once. There are layers upon layers of pain, old traumas overlaid by new ones. This work proceeds spiral-wise; there will be periods of remission, when the hurt fades and your attention is given to other things, and then it will present itself once more.

Finally, just as you need help to find your way in to your feelings, so you may need help in knowing when you have done enough to honour them. It is possible to get hooked on intensity, to find a kind of joy in fierce anger or deep grieving that can be hard to let go of, especially if you have cherished these feelings in your heart for many years. They make you feel real and alive; without them, what will you be?

I have been working for the last year or so with Martha, who is in her mid-twenties. When she was a young child she was sexually abused by her father, and she left home as soon as she could and broke off all contact with her family. Towards her father, she felt an intense rage and hatred. When she heard that he was dying, she rejoiced. He contacted her, wanting to make peace before he died, but Martha's reaction was one of contempt and furious rejection; let him suffer as she had suffered.

One day, Martha brought with her a letter that her father had written. Until then, we had been following her feelings as they arose, and it seemed clear that she was far from ready to forgive. As I read the letter, however, a new picture of her father began to emerge. He wrote that he was truly sorry, that he was appalled at the damage he had caused and that if he could live his life again, things would be very different. There was no self-justification, nothing for Martha to hang her anger upon; simply a very moving appeal, not for her forgiveness, but for some kind of meeting before it was too late.

The letter seemed to me to be a statement of genuine repentance. Martha was furious, as usual, but it struck me that there was a hollow quality to her anger; she was clinging to it, wrapping it around her like a protective cloak. Protective against what? In asking the question, the answer became clear. Without her rage, who would she be? Behind the anger was terror.

It was a turning point in our work together, and the beginning of a new task; the building of a Martha who was much more than an abused and grievously wounded child. She did go to see her father, for she felt now that if she did not, she would carry regret for the rest of her life. There was no Hollywood-style scene of last-minute reconciliation as he lay on his deathbed, but now that she was finding new ground to stand on where she was not his victim, they were able to meet, and there was healing in it for both of them.

3. BREAKING NEW GROUND

Martha's story also illustrates another aspect of the forgiveness process. At the same time as you are giving your pain the attention that it deserves, you also need to expand your life into other areas that are untouched by old wounds. This is not as paradoxical as it sounds. It does not mean finding distractions and trying to forget about it. Instead, it means making a conscious choice to widen your options, to strengthen the fragile, often almost stifled self that says that this is not all of who you are; that there is much more to you than being a victim.

As you work to create new spaces in your life, so you reduce the impact of the wounding, and you allow yourself to be nourished in whatever you choose to do. Little by little, this paves the way for the grace to come to you that will finally enable you to forgive.

4. CONSCIOUS FORGIVENESS

Sometimes, as you proceed with the work of honouring your feelings and widening your horizons – Steps 2 and 3 – forgiveness comes about gently, of its own accord.

This happened for Rose, a client of mine who had been working for two years or so on the damage done to her by her father, who had physically and sexually abused her. To begin with, she had nothing but dark memories of her childhood. She painted a picture of constant bickering between her parents, rising unpredictably to violent rage, and she remembered no affectionate physical contact at all.

The intensity of her unlocked feelings had begun to diminish, and Rose was taking a break from therapy for a few months – focusing instead on 'real life', as she put it – when she began, unexpectedly, to recall memories that had a different flavour; moments of good parenting. They were accompanied by feelings of tenderness towards her father, with the understanding that he had been, in his way, no less a victim than she herself. She realised with some surprise that she had forgiven him.

You cannot, however, count on this happening. If you have come to the point where you actively want to forgive, but know that you cannot quite let go, a ritual of some kind can help you to go through that last barrier. It is important to devise it yourself, or to take some part in creating it, so that you forgive exactly as much as you choose, and in your own way. It can be solitary, or you can use witnesses or other participants.

Ritual is a very potent tool for transformation. It provides containment, a focusing for your intentions and your actions, and it acknowledges the power of spirit, your own and whatever higher powers you choose to call upon, to take you through when you can't manage on your own. It can be as simple as a prayer, or a symbolic act of letting go, such as burying or burning something that represents the past; or it can be as elaborate as your imagination allows.

I have been working with Vicky, who is sixteen years old. Three years ago her mother killed herself, and since then Vicky had been in a frozen state, unable to grieve because of her suppressed rage, and unable to rage because of her terrible guilt. Together we set up a ritual in which she brought a picture of her mother and lit a candle in front of it. The only instruction was that she was to talk to her mother, and to allow whatever feelings came up without censorship. Because we had created a sacred space, removed from the everyday world, Vicky was at last able to let herself be with her feelings in a way that had not been possible for her with her family, her friends or myself as her counsellor. It was clear to her that she needed to forgive her mother for taking her own life, and with the help of the ritual she was able to begin to do this.

5. AFTER FORGIVENESS

How do you know when you have truly forgiven? It is easy to pretend to yourself, because you want to be generous and loving, but if there is still resentment, if old scores still come up when you are feeling vulnerable, then you have not forgiven. The mark of forgiveness, as Rose discovered, is when other and softer feelings arise. Sometimes you can't even recall what you felt any more; the energy invested there has been freed and put to other uses.

More often, however, you are left with a mixture of feelings, and the hallmark of forgiveness is not so much that the hurt or anger is gone for good, as that it no longer hooks you; you can feel it, acknowledge it and move on. Then you are as free as you can ever be from the tangles of the past, and available for intimate relationship in the here and now.

In summary

The focus of this chapter is on practical ways to manage conflict in your relationship: how to minimise it by looking after yourself, how to understand what is happening when you do come into conflict and how to handle conflicts so that your relationship is not damaged but strengthened. Also covered is how wounding from the past can 'leak' into your present relationship, and how letting go of old wounds, or forgiving, can help you be more fully present. Next we move on to the subject of sex and the problems you may encounter in this area once you are in a relationship.

Chapter 7
Let's Talk About Sex

**Only the united best of heart and sex together
can create ecstacy.**
> Anais Nin, French writer, 1903–1977

Does it seem a little strange to get this far into a book about intimate relationships with hardly a mention of sex? Isn't sex at the centre of any partnership?

Think about the couples you know. Of those who've been together more than a year or so, how many do you know who don't really get on very well, but still have great sex? It's possible to desire someone without liking them, but the odds are against it developing into a long-term relationship. On the other hand, think of the couples you know who have settled into partnerships that are warm and comfortable, full of affection and shared pleasures – but who don't make love much any more. Sex may start out at the centre of some partnerships, but it tends not to stay there. If your emotional life is not flowing, or distance has grown between you and your partner, then sex is often the first casualty.

This is only a problem if you feel you're not getting enough, or if it's become boring when you do have sex – or, of course, if you start to fancy someone else and your relationship is suddenly in danger. These are all areas we'll be looking at in this chapter. Even for the couple who are perfectly content, however, going through life side by side and occasionally making love, it can be dangerous to assume that all is well and nothing needs to change. Sexual energy is an unpredictable force. At times it can seem to disappear altogether, and at other times it can erupt like a volcano, bringing chaos to the best-ordered lives. Any relationship can benefit from a review now and then, and the more you are aware of how well met – or not – you feel in your relationship, the less likely you are to be taken off guard by unexpected problems.

Not getting enough?

The first question to be asked here is whether you both wish you were having more sex, or whether it is only one of you who thinks there is a problem. If it's both of you, then at least there is common ground to start with. There is no mileage in exploring ways to liven up your sex life together if one partner is holding back either openly or secretly. We'll look at that side of things later. For now, let's look at the possibilities for you both, as a couple, to make some changes. You can start by doing the following exercise.

Exercise 18
Making space for sex

STEP 1
Come together with your partner in the usual way. You will each need a pen and some paper. Take some time to consider the following questions:

Is there enough time for lovemaking? Is it simply that with all the other demands in your lives, sex is being squeezed out? List the things that have to be done. Looking after children is a big one, especially when they are small, perhaps waking at night, interrupting your privacy and maybe sleeping in your bed. The demands of work may mean that one or both of you gets home late and tired, wanting only to fall into bed and go to sleep. There may be other things, too, that get in the way.

Is it hard to find a time when you are both ready and willing? It may be that you used to enjoy making love in the morning, but children and work now rule that out. Or perhaps you are still hopeful by the time you go to bed but your partner is exhausted?

What about the quality of your lovemaking? When you do manage to make love, are you satisfied with what you do, or has it become routine, or even boring?

STEP 2

Set aside some time to share what you have written. Take it in turns at first to speak, and then to listen. Notice where the two of you are in agreement, and where you differ. Notice also where your partner gives more emphasis to some aspect of the situation than you would do. There is a great deal of potential for change in these differences, so listen carefully. When you have an ordinary conversation with your partner you may have been discounting them or editing them out simply because they do not fit with your own views. Now, as you listen, give them extra weight; make a note when you hear something like this – especially when it makes you feel uncomfortable.

STEP 3

Now you have something to work with. First, identify the areas of complete agreement. For instance, it may be that you both recognise that there is not enough time for lovemaking. Given that you want to make more space for it, how can you do this? You may need to create the space by moving aside other things. Perhaps you can do this by coming home early from work, taking a long lunch break or leaving the children with a minder until after tea – you will find your own windows of opportunity. The point is that if you want to do this you are going to have to find space and then keep it open, otherwise it will get filled up. When you were footloose and fancy free there was no problem. Now you are a couple with many items on the agenda, and sex can easily fall to the bottom of the list. It takes effort to stop this from happening.

STEP 4

Look at the areas of difference. First, take it in turns to acknowledge what you heard your partner say, so that they know they have not been ignored. If you found some things difficult to hear, say so.

STEP 5

When you have both spoken, take turns to speak again. When it is your turn, choose one or two of the issues that came up for your partner, and say what you can offer to help resolve them. Don't try to tackle everything at once; willingness is more than half the battle. Choose things initially that you immediately feel moved by. For instance, if your partner said something like 'After I've fed the children, bathed them, read their stories and put them to bed, I've got no energy left for sex', you could offer to take over some of those tasks. If your partner in turn undertakes to do something relaxing and refreshing with the time that is freed up – whatever that may be – you will both gain by this. Be careful not to fall into the traps of blame and resentment. This exercise is structured to allow you to make offers, not demands.

STEP 6

Arrange a time to try out the changes you've agreed on, within the next week if possible. Before you finish, also set up a time to review the situation. Again, don't leave it too long – probably two weeks at most. Thank each other, and close the exercise.

Identifying the places where you could create space for love-making and making a firm commitment to doing this is the first step towards rekindling an active sex life. Beware of self-sabotage, however. The part of you that believes sex should be spontaneous, that planning and passion don't mix, may try to trip you up. When it comes to the point, watch out for the urge to say 'I'm too tired' or 'I don't feel like it now.' Being spontaneous in the past has led to less sex, or even no sex, so you have to get beyond this one. Consider the following scenario:

Imagine you are meeting your secret lover at 4 o'clock. You have both had to work at creating this time to meet, and no one knows about it but the two of you. You will only have forty minutes. Imagine how you will get ready, the clothes you will wear, the excitement as you reach your agreed meeting place. Is it likely that when it comes to the point, your desire will suddenly desert you?

Now use your imagination to carry you towards your date with your partner. After all, it really is a secret meeting, at a time stolen from other duties. This is your lover, the one you have chosen to spend your life with, and sex between you is a joyful expression of your intimacy. Build in the need for planning and timing, just as you would if you were having an affair; make it part of the game. Play it right and what looked like a passion-killer can actually add to the intensity of your meetings.

Sex is boring

If making space is the first step towards more and better sex, the second step is to look again at the third question in the last exercise (*see page 129*). Do you feel that sex has become boring and routine? As long as you are both willing, there is plenty of scope for improvement here too.

When you are first together, excited and passionate about each other, you will do things in bed – and out of it – that take both of you beyond your usual limits, and perhaps beyond anything you have experienced before. As time goes on, however, and your blood cools, the range and intensity of your lovemaking tends to diminish. You come to know and trust each other, and to say when you find some things less pleasurable than others. Little by little, without either of you really intending this, your sex life sinks to the lowest common denominator – what you both like, or don't mind, and what is easy. Add to that the need to be quiet, and maybe quick as well if children are around, and it's not surprising that what you end up with is hardly enough to make your heart beat faster.

There are countless manuals on how to spice up your sex life, endless advice on technique, clothes to buy and equipment to try out; you will never get to the end of it all. With willingness and a sense of adventure, you can go as far as you like. If you have started by making more time for sex, you can also make an agreement to use that time to explore beyond your usual familiar patterns. Before embarking on new adventures, it is worth going back to basics. There are two important points to bear in mind here.

The first is that being in love, or at least in lust, carries you into new places, and takes you way beyond what you would do in cold blood. Perhaps more for women than men, love is what opens the way to wonderful sex. Feeling loved and desired is a turn-on in itself, but feeling desired without love can be a definite turn-off. It's no good saying, 'But of course I love you, now let's get on with it.'

Seducers succeed because they know how to manipulate the object of their desire into feeling loved. They put effort into setting the scene, giving their partner the attention that makes them glow – and women know how to do this just as much as men. The dishonesty of seduction is that the seducer is only after part of the deal, using love as a lure to get sex, or sex as a lure to get power. In your relationship, however, you have signed up for the whole deal, so use the language of seduction to make your partner feel special. You will both reap the rewards.

The second point is that although sex techniques are not really as important for a good love life as the sex manuals seem to suggest, they do matter. If the base line is feeling 'up for it', and part of feeling up for it is feeling loved and desired, then that includes knowing that your partner is willing to do what you like. It is also important that he or she notices when you don't like something.

In the normal run of things, it's not easy to say too much about your partner's performance when you are in the middle of lovemaking. It kills passion, and brings in anger and shame and a whole mess of emotions that belong on the darker side of sexuality. So you tend not to mention it when you haven't enjoyed something, but then you have to carry your resentment and frustration and feeling uncared for. If these things stay unacknowledged, they can build up to a point where you both come to lovemaking feeling anxious, knowing that your partner isn't really with you, and you both go away feeling let down – again – and disappointed. With all that going on, no wonder your sex life has dwindled.

Other people's bodies are a mystery, whether your partner is of the opposite sex or not, and it takes time to learn the ways of pleasure. It takes time to develop trust and openness, especially if, in the first delight of meeting, you have let things pass that really do not work for you. In bed more than in any other area of relationship, you often expect your partner to be telepathic, or at least superbly tuned in to your needs and responses. Sometimes it happens that way, but more often you need to work at it. You have to allow yourself to be taught, as well as to perform; and if you have something to teach, you have to learn to do it gently, playfully, with generosity – not 'You're doing it wrong!' but 'That doesn't really work for me. How about trying this?'

The next exercise, then, is about reading each other's signals. If there is a backlog of unexpressed feelings between you, this can be a tricky one. You are going to try to change things without talking and analysing; instead of picking apart what you've been doing wrong, you are going to start doing it right. If there is love and willingness between you, you can leave the mistakes of the past behind, and move forward into a much more satisfying sex life.

Exercise 19
Reading each other's needs

STEP 1
Arrange your time and place as usual, making absolutely sure that you will not be interrupted by the phone, children or anything else. Before you begin the exercise, take time to make

the room beautiful. Use candles or soft lighting, and throws to cover up ugly or distracting things, and transform the space into somewhere that invites erotic play. Have ready whatever you think you might want later – massage oils, finger foods, wine or whatever comes to mind. Prepare yourself as if you were meeting a new lover: bathe, clean your teeth and dress so that you feel and look attractive and sexy.

STEP 2

Come together at the appointed time. Each of you in turn will have a period of time – half an hour at least – in which your partner will be at your service, giving you pleasure in whatever way you choose. This can include anything that takes your fancy, but don't move into actual intercourse. This exercise is about expanding erotic energy, and all too often when your sex life has dwindled, penetrative sex can be all that's left.

Agree who is to go first, then that person will take five minutes to say what you would like your partner to do. You might want only to be massaged or held, or perhaps given a bath or fed with fruit. You might want more directly sexual touching. Be as specific as you can beforehand, so that you do not need to speak once the exercise has begun. The task of the listener is to listen well and do their best to please their partner. If you are asked to do something that makes you feel uncomfortable, say so, but otherwise your partner is in command.

STEP 3

Now take your half hour or however much time you have. The giving partner needs to be aware of the time. As you are receiving give your partner feedback without words; use your body to show your pleasure. When something is less pleasurable, you can indicate that by tensing up or going still. Help your partner to notice how you are feeling, and your partner, in turn, will be looking for cues. If you want something else or something different, guide your partner's hands; try not to use words unless you have to. If it goes well it becomes a kind of dance, and both of you will get pleasure from the exchange.

STEP 4
Take a little time if you like to lie together quietly, then swap roles. Now it is your turn to give. Be as open as you can; try to leave aside what you think you know about your partner's likes and dislikes, and watch for cues in the here and now. Notice what they ask and do not ask for. Imagine that this person is someone you really want to please.

STEP 5
When the time is up, lie down together and thank each other in whatever way feels appropriate. Give each other feedback, but be careful not to criticise or blame. Praising what you enjoyed is much more constructive than passing judgment on your partner's technique. If you have enjoyed yourselves, agree on a time to do this again. Half an hour is not very long, and there will be many more things to try. As your confidence grows that your partner will notice your cues and respect them, and also that they will ask for what they want instead of leaving you to guess, so you will both be freed up to be more adventurous if you choose.

You may want to move into lovemaking if you haven't already. On the other hand, you may want to stay with what you have learned and experienced for now. Unless you both want to make love, don't; there is no pressure to go anywhere with this exercise. It is about expansion, rather than about going down the same old tracks, so it may be more useful to leave it at that for now.

Sex games

By now if things are going well you should both be feeling a lot more hopeful and excited about your sex life. A sense that new possibilities are opening up and your horizons are widening allows you to approach the whole topic of sex with confidence and a sense of playfulness. This is an essential quality to cultivate if you want to banish boredom. Even if you can only manage the time and energy to do something special every so often, the times in between will be fine because you know a treat is on the way. It's like going out for a special meal now and then or having the occasional weekend away; ordinary days are livable when you don't have them all the time.

This next exercise is an invitation to play, to go beyond your normal limits and surprise yourself and your partner. You can do it as many times as you like.

Exercise 20
Playing games

STEP 1
Come together as usual, and prepare the room and yourselves as you did for the previous exercise (*see pages 133–4*). You may be taking the exercise outside this time and place, but put as much energy into it as before. You are going to take it in turns to be in charge, but only one of you will get your turn this time, so choose who will go first.

If it is your turn, you are the master or the mistress of ceremonies. You will give the orders, although if your partner feels uncomfortable about anything they are, of course, allowed to refuse. Ask for what you want, and be prepared to negotiate. You may want to stay in the room, or choose another stage – it could be outdoors, in a restaurant, at the cinema, wherever takes your fancy. Use your imagination; this is a game, and no one is judging you or telling you off. You call the shots. Perhaps there is something you have fantasised about doing, or perhaps you need to start fantasising now.

Make your instructions as specific as you can. Choose what your partner will wear, and tell them exactly what you want them to do. It could be directly sexual, or more subtle and indirect, at least at first. In this exercise you will be able to speak if you need to, although you may ask your partner not to talk. Instructions or orders may be part of the game.

STEP 2

Let the play begin. It may not be possible to do it immediately, depending on what you have in mind. Let the anticipation be part of the game. When you do move into the second step, make sure you have enough time to let the play develop; it may take an evening, half a day or even longer. It may be that, during the next week, your partner will do whatever you tell them when you tell them (phones can be useful for this one). This is not really about dominance and submission, although you could choose to explore that road. It's about expanding the space in which you can express your sexuality and allowing yourselves to be taken beyond your usual limits in an atmosphere of trust and playfulness. However long it takes, make sure you also agree on the finishing time.

STEP 3

Come together again, and give feedback. As usual, avoid blaming. If your partner was honest about saying no, they should not feel pushed too far. Perhaps some things didn't work too well. That's fine; you've learned something useful. Perhaps some things were wonderful, better than you expected. Celebrate that. Finish by arranging a time for your partner to have their turn before too long.

What if you don't agree?

So far we have looked at what you can do if both of you agree that your sex life needs livening up. It's quite common, however, to find that one of you wants more sex, while the other is apparently happy with the way things are. If that is your story, the first thing you need to do is to put your emotional house in order. If, between the two of you, you have built up a backlog of resentments and hurts, one of the things that tends to suffer is the flow of sexual energy. In other words, if you don't feel warm towards your partner, you don't want to make love with them. It tends to be women more than men who 'go off' sex in this way, partly because women tend to be more heart-focused, and partly because men tend to neglect their emotional house-keeping and assume it's all fine until – inexplicably – their partner refuses to make love. Consider the following story.

> Mark was a client of mine who was full of anger and frustra-tion because his wife, Lisa, hardly ever wanted to make love. I asked him to describe a typical day in their household and he spoke of working at full stretch, coming home exhausted, dealing with children and supper, and having very little space for himself. Meanwhile, Lisa was also working part-time, looking after their two young children – one of whom was still breastfeeding – and running the house. At the end of the day, usually when she was in the bathroom getting ready for bed, he would approach her, try to give her a hug and ask to make love. Lisa, knowing what was coming, would stiffen as he touched her, and then say that she was very tired and didn't feel like it. He would retreat, angry and rejected, and she would withdraw into herself.
>
> Does this sound familiar? I certainly remember similar scenes with my own wife when the children were small. Here were two people, both pushed to their limits, neither getting enough support from each other or from anywhere else. Between them ran a river of resentment, hurt feelings and unmet needs, and it was getting wider. Is it any wonder that Lisa, who was less able or willing to split her emotional and sexual selves than Mark was, should not want to make love with him?

We have all been here if we have been in relationship for any length of time. It happens when communication starts to dry up, when we begin to feel hard done by, or to take each other for granted. It is usually, though not always, women who lead the way, because women tend to find it harder to flow sexually when their hearts are not in it. However, there is something even worse than not making love when you don't feel like it. Many times I have counselled women who say, 'I don't really want to make love with my husband, but I feel I ought to.' Once a week or once a month or whatever, they perform their marital duty. This is quite simply horrible. It is a kind of self-violation for the woman and, needless to say, it does nothing to bring you closer together. If this is your situation, it is yet another invitation to wake up, to begin the work of relationship.

Sexuality does not exist in isolation; rather, it comes to serve as a kind of barometer of the emotional health of a partnership. If you do not begin to attend to your emotional needs, the sexual meeting between you and your partner will also suffer. It is normal and natural for this to happen. In fact, it is part of the process of moving closer together, rather than a sign that things are falling apart – although, if you are not willing to go with the process of heart opening, you may choose to take it that way.

When we approach each other sexually, we have to learn how to come from a place of fullness rather than neediness. Looking to another to meet our needs may be all right for a while and as long as we do not want to go deep, but in the long term *it does not work*. It is only when we have healed ourselves enough and developed our own inner resources enough, that we can truly come together. Then, relationship happens delightfully, creatively, arising from the overflow of energy between us. Rather than grasping at each other to try to fill our emptiness, we can truly dance together.

If this is where you are, go back to the earlier chapters of the book. As you work through some of the exercises with your partner and the two of you begin to be able to speak – and to hear – some of the hurt between you, so healing will happen. And as your hearts open to each other, sexual energy will begin to flow again.

No sex drive at all?

In one of the tabloid papers recently I saw an article about a couple who were both well-known actors. The headline screamed, 'No sex for a year!' as though this were one of the biggest disasters that can befall a partnership. In fact, periods when our sexual energy seems to disappear or go underground are very common, whether we are in a relationship or not.

This happens for a variety of reasons. Obviously, some kinds of physical illness affect our libido, and so does clinical depression. A major trauma, such as a bereavement or an operation, can cause it to disappear; and being a victim of sexual abuse, whether as a child or as an adult, is a common cause. In fact, being a victim of violence in any form, from seeing active service in the armed forces to having a car accident – anything that is, or seems to be, beyond our control – can lead to loss of libido.

In all of these examples, while there is work to be done to heal the trauma, we also have to accept that the body has its own wisdom, and that it is necessary to be abstinent for a time. There may be no obvious cause, and yet it happens, and it is something that we must make space for in a committed relationship.

As we have seen, the most likely time for celibacy to become an issue between partners is when they start a family. It is very common and completely normal for a woman to lose interest in sex, even sometimes for two or three years after she has had a baby. In many tribal societies this is recognised and respected, yet in the Western world it is one of the factors that often leads to the breakdown of a marriage. In becoming a mother, a woman is forced to grow up rapidly, learning to stretch her resources beyond her previous limits. One of the things that can happen is that for a varying length of time, her vital and hence sexual energy becomes focused upon her child rather than upon her partner. There may well be survival value for the child in this, in that it delays the arrival of younger siblings.

Whatever the reason for it, letting it become a focus for anger and resentment between you simply adds to all the other burdens. The best thing a man can do in this situation is to be loving and supportive, take as much of the load as he can, and call in support from friends, childminders, cleaners – whatever it takes to allow the woman the time and space to replenish herself. What is the alternative? Start an affair, leave the marriage and end up playing a minimal part in the lives of your children. If you put energy in, you will – in the long run – get it back many times over.

Jealousy: the green-eyed monster

Why is jealousy seen as a monster? Because it takes you over, makes you behave in monstrous and destructive ways, and bears no resemblance to love. It has everything to do with your own insecurity and desire to control your partner, and nothing to do with mature, honest and mutually supportive relationships. And sometimes it is entirely justified. Consider the following two stories.

My friend Philip has a whole string of women friends with whom he has occasional sex. He is the envy of his mates, who see him as a pretty laid-back guy. Recently, he met Ellie, newly divorced and looking for fun. She liked to go clubbing, was seeing two men now and then, and was quite clear that she did not want to move into a committed relationship any time soon.

Philip was fine with this at first, and they went out a few times. He found himself falling in love with her and, despite the clear messages she gave him, pressed her to give up her other men and be with him. When she withdrew he started to bombard her with phone calls and text messages. She liked him and found it hard to push him away altogether, but this only fed his hope – or fantasy – that one day she would be his. He knew his behaviour was likely to produce exactly the opposite result, but he said he could not help himself. It all ended catastrophically when he went to her house one evening, convinced that another man was with her. When she would not let him in, he put his fist through a window.

What was all that about? All Philip's friends told him he was mad and should stop all contact with Ellie, but he could not do it. This is a clear example of the power of projection, in which Philip's inner world had completely obscured his view of the real, flesh-and-blood woman who was so obviously not the woman of his dreams. He didn't mind that all the other women he was seeing had lives of their own, but something about Ellie made him want her for himself alone.

Stories like this are the stuff of plays and poetry, high drama and soap opera, but the reality is usually wretched for everyone concerned. Weaning yourself off jealousy can be as hard as coming off drugs, but if you really do want to be in a close and loving relationship, you have to do it for your life's sake. You will need strong friends and maybe professional support too. If you are already in a partnership, there is work you can do with your partner; we explore some possibilities below. Here now is the second story.

Faye came to me for therapy because she was afraid she was going mad. She was a lively and attractive woman who had been married for ten years and had a three-year-old daughter. She told me that in the last two and a half years or so she had become obsessed with the notion that her husband was having an affair. She would check his emails, open his letters, examine his clothes and ring him up at odd times. She found no evidence at all, and her husband was furious with her. He told her she was mad, and she was unable to justify herself. Could it be some form of psychosis after childbirth?

About six months into therapy there came a breakthrough. She found a letter from her husband's lover and when she confronted him with it, he admitted everything. The affair had begun exactly when she thought, and with the woman whom she suspected. Her husband could no longer stand the tension and had accidentally left the letter where he knew she would find it. He had betrayed her in two ways – by being unfaithful and by teaching her to doubt her own sanity. Trying to contain all of this had brought him close to a breakdown himself.

What links these two stories? Obviously, there are similarities in the way that Philip and Faye felt and behaved. Both were told they were mad by those closest to them. Both felt driven by the fear that the object of their jealousy was not being faithful to them – and in both cases, as it turned out, this fear was entirely justified. But jealousy needs no justification; it can be just as intense when there is no cause at all. It is always an invitation to call your projections home.

Get whatever support you can to help you understand what drives you to behave in such a love-destroying way, and to work on changing it. Philip was trying to do this by talking with his friends; Faye had sought help through therapy only to discover that her 'madness' was really intuition that was being denied. And here is the crucial difference between the two stories. Philip had no justification for his jealousy, no right to expect anything from Ellie. Faye and her husband, on the other hand, had made vows to each other and her jealousy was telling her something that she needed to know.

We will look in more depth at what happens when people who are supposedly committed to each other are unfaithful, but for now we need to find some ways to handle jealousy within a partnership. If it really is a monster, how can you start to tame it?

If you are in a committed relationship, the first step is to reassure each other that this means exactly what it says. In other words, whoever else you may be attracted to, you are not going to leave your partner. Put a term on it if that helps to make it easier. Relationships are constantly changing, and it makes sense to review your contract every so often; so you can say, for example, 'I will not sleep with anyone else in the next year.' This doesn't mean you will go off with someone else as soon as the year is up! What it does is to give you both some solid ground to stand on. Then your feelings of jealousy can be held and explored between the two of you as they arise.

Jealousy is a monster because it comes from a very deep and primitive part of you, a childlike place in which any threat to your ownership of your loved one seems like a threat to your whole existence. It overwhelms the rational part of you because it comes from your gut, not your head. The only way to tame it is to not deny it; not to pretend you're just fine and can cope. Nor does it help to indulge it, to extract promises from your partner so that you can feel secure. Jealousy feeds on itself, and if you allow it to make the rules, you will box your relationship into a dark corner where it will eventually wither away for lack of light and air. The only way to start to grow beyond jealousy is to welcome it in, to befriend it like a wild creature that has never learned to trust people.

How can you do that? First, by making a pact with your partner that you will be open about times when you feel jealous. Notice any incident, however small, from smiling at a shopkeeper to apparently getting off with someone else, which activates your insecurity. Bring it to your partner in the exercise below.

Exercise 21
Taming the monster

STEP 1

Come together and take turns to speak as usual. Jealousy may not be an issue for both of you, but use the space to speak about anything that has come up for you during the day. If there is something that made you feel jealous, talk about what happened for you. Speak about yourself and your feelings, not about what your partner might or might not have been doing or feeling. This is about you, not about them.

STEP 2

When you listen, don't interrupt or try to explain. Just be there for your partner; feel what they felt, and let them see that you are acknowledging their pain. A jealous person is in torment and the thing they need most is the sense that they are loved. What you actually did or said is pretty much irrelevant – unless you really are breaking the promise you made. If you are being unfaithful in some way, your partner will certainly know, at some level, and will not be reassured. If you are not, just be there for them.

STEP 3

Finish with some quiet time; holding or touching in some way is important here. There is no need to analyse whatever happened; if there is love between you, allowing that to flow means that you can let go of the incident rather than giving it more energy.

Once these basic structures are in place – a promise not to leave, and a promise to talk about jealous moments – you can start to transform the monster. In time, you can not only tame it, but also play with it, make it your friend and ally. Instead of threatening your relationship, it can enhance and expand it.

The truth is, no matter how committed to each other you are, you cannot own each other's sexuality. A person who never noticed other people would be seriously disabled in their engagement with the world. Sexual cues are part of what we pick up about a person without even being aware of it, and we respond to them in an unconscious way as well. You behave differently with someone when you find them attractive than when you do not; you can't help it. Sexuality is part of the colour and flavour of our interactions with each other; without it, life would be a dreary business. And when you bring it into consciousness, when you flirt with someone, it lifts you both, reaffirms you as attractive beings, sends you on your way feeling good. So instead of pretending it doesn't happen and drawing a circle that shuts out everyone except you and your partner, bring it in. Celebrate each other's ability to attract and be attracted. After all, it is what brought you together in the first place.

Try the following exercise.

Exercise 22
Out to play

STEP 1
For this exercise you need to be somewhere public, where you can talk without being overheard. A pub or a bar is a good place, as is a restaurant – not too quiet – or somewhere outdoors like the beach or the park.

STEP 2
Look at the people around you. Who do you find attractive? Point them out to your partner – not too obviously, of course. Talk about what it is that attracts you. It may be something

physical – their hair, their breasts, their figure in general – or it may be how they seem in other ways. Are they laughing with friends or brooding alone in a corner? Do they seem confident, happy, serious, dangerous? Elaborate on what you notice; make up a story about them if you like. Build on it together. If you happen to catch their eye, give them a smile. Let them know you appreciate them. It doesn't mean you have to take them home, after all; you are sitting here with your loved one, and this is about your shared sexuality.

STEP 3
Notice if feelings of jealousy come up and say if they do, but do not allow them to sabotage the game. Bring them along, but don't indulge them. If this goes well, it will start to nibble away at the territory where jealousy rules. Instead of it being a no-go area, it becomes a place of shared pleasure and another way to add spice to your sex life.

Once you start to admit your responses to the people around you and share them with your partner, you can take it as far as you like. For every couple trying to live within the constricting coils of jealousy, there are plenty more couples who love to see their partner glowing more brightly as they drink in the admiration of other men and women. If you let it, it can be a source of nourishment and pleasure in your relationship. And the irony of it is that you – and your partner – are less likely to be unfaithful to each other when you don't have to hide your attractions to other people. Unfaithfulness is another story, and that is the subject of the next section.

Dealing with infidelity

The first thing to get straight, as we have seen above, is that there is really no such thing as total fidelity. Who has not admired a good-looking man or a beautiful woman as they walked by? Who has not fantasised about a film star, someone at work, their next-door neighbour? The Bill Clinton definition of 'sexual relations' as penetrative sex can never be taken seriously again. Sexual energy can be exchanged in a look, a touch or a silence between two people. If there is a charge in the air, almost anything can both feed and express it: eating together, dancing together or just walking side by side. Some of the most erotic moments in films are ones like these, as all good film directors know. Actual scenes of lovemaking can be a bit of a letdown – as can lovemaking in real life, of course.

So far, so good. Most people will be able to do Exercise 22 without too much trouble. But where do you draw the line? What if your partner's eyes are continually wandering, and they no longer want to make love to you any more? What if you suspect, or actually know, that they are seeing someone else? What if you are the one who wants to have an affair?

There are no hard and fast rules here. What works for one couple may be torture for another. The only rule for a strong and secure relationship is that both of you should agree on what your boundaries are. In a great many marriages it is understood that there will be no infidelity. In many more, it is understood – but not spoken – that if either or both of you does have affairs, you will take care not to be found out. In others, affairs are openly acknowledged and even approved. In a few, the so-called 'open relationships', the couple will talk about their sexual adventures to each other, and even share sexual partners.

In general, people become more relaxed about their boundaries as they get older. The myth of 'happy ever after' tends to wear thin and what really works for us takes over. What is not all right, however, is to pretend that you are being faithful because that is what your partner wants, when you are not – whatever definition of 'faithful' you are using. That way lies deceit and betrayal, heartache and destruction. It is the way of soap opera, and if you and your partner really care about your relationship – as you presumably do if you have got this far through the book – it will not do. If one of you wants sex elsewhere and the other is not happy about it, your relationship is doomed. It could continue, as many marriages do, for the rest of your lives, but you can never have true and strong intimacy between you. That is a bargain that plenty of people make, but it is not the kind of relationship we have been considering here.

This does not mean that your relationship cannot grow and change, and take lessons from past affairs. Learning to gain strength from tough times is one of the challenges of a mature relationship.

> Justin and Karen met and fell in love when they were teenagers, and when they married she had never slept with anyone else. After a few years, her lack of sexual experience began to worry her; what was she missing? She began an affair with an older man. When Justin found out, he was devastated.
>
> The marriage almost ended then and there, as it often does. Instead, they began to look at what had gone wrong. Justin realised that he had stopped communicating with her in any meaningful way and was taking her place in his life for granted. Although he never left physically, he was emotionally absent. Instead of blaming her, he admitted his share of responsibility. On her part, Karen felt met by Justin for the first time in quite a while. She also saw and acknowledged how much pain he was in. They worked intensively on their relationship for many months, and eventually recommitted themselves to each other. The new relationship between them was much deeper and stronger than the old one, and it has continued to grow. They have just celebrated their silver wedding anniversary.

Once again, it comes down to good communication. Forget about having a secret affair, however exciting and fabulous the sex is. At some level, if you are tuned into each other at all your partner will always know. It is far more fruitful, in the long run, to work at bringing in your sexuality. Share your desires and fantasies with each other. If it feels safe to you, act on them, and keep communicating with your partner. The more you do this, the stronger and richer your emotional life together will be, and the less likely you will be to go looking for emotional fulfilment, as well as sex, elsewhere.

In summary

In this chapter we have focused on some of the most likely sexual problems that you may encounter as you get into a relationship, and as you try to stay there. We've looked at boredom, loss of sex drive, jealousy and infidelity, and suggested ways in which you can try to turn these potential marriage wreckers into allies, things that can actually feed and enrich your sexual and emotional life together instead of destroying it. The next chapter brings together all the relationship skills we have discussed so far, and asks what a mature relationship looks like.

Chapter 8
Towards Mature Relationships

There is no greater risk, perhaps, than matrimony, but there is nothing happier than a happy marriage.
Benjamin Disraeli, British Prime Minister
and writer, 1804–1881

There is no blueprint for what we are trying to create. Our only touchstone is our own humanity. As the old structures of family and religion fall away, we are being forced to find wisdom within ourselves. If we are to make relationships that are strong and lasting, that can hold us in our joy and in our pain, in our ecstasy and in our despair, and in all the less exciting places in between, we must learn to weave them from the substance of our own hearts and souls. There is no room for what we think we ought to be, but only for what we are.

What we are and what we have the potential to be is far more wonderful than any of the fantasies we can conjure up. It is a necessary part of making a relationship that we start out with a picture of the other that is embroidered partly from reality and partly from our own fantasies. Equally, it becomes necessary to let go of the fantasies, to be disillusioned. As we do this, as we learn to accept the reality of the other, so we free ourselves, and them, to unfold more of our potential.

It gets easier to take all this on board as you get older. In fact, in this day and age it is probably wise not to settle into a committed relationship at all – and in particular, not to have children – before your late twenties at least. Marriages made in the teens and twenties are very likely to end in divorce, and no one would dispute the trauma this causes to the children, even if the wounds appear to heal with time. Nowadays, young adulthood is a time for exploring, gaining experience and beginning to understand your patterns and limitations through having many partners. If you 'settle down' too young, you may well need to break out later in your life.

The thirties and forties is the time when most relationships move on into having children if they are going to, simply because of biological necessity. It is also the time when a lot of people come into therapy, or go through some sort of mid-life crisis; having made their mark on life, it is now time to take stock, to leave behind what doesn't work so well and try new things. This can, of course, mean new partners as well, or it can mean re-evaluating the established partnerships. A lot of the stories in this book come from this age group.

What about the fifties and sixties, and beyond? Nowadays, we hope to stay outgoing and sexually active, forming new friendships and relationships, right up until the end of our lives. Quite right, too. If you've got to this stage with a partner, you'll have seen each other in illness, under stress, in grief and at a loss. You have to contend with physical changes, with the menopause and other signs of ageing; the fear of becoming unattractive, and the fear of disability and death. You become more humble, ready to accept imperfection in yourself and in your partner. What looks unromantic in your twenties – comfort, familiarity, steadiness – becomes in fact the key to a good relationship.

You also come to value your family and friends more highly. If you are wise, you take care to build and maintain a network that extends beyond the two of you, and includes people of different age groups and interests from your own. If sex happens less frequently, it can also become more special – particularly for women, who have the chance to step beyond the restrictions of the child-bearing years and enjoy their sexuality without shame. By the time you are in your seventies, with a bit of luck you will have outlived the old rules altogether, like my friend Edith. She is now seventy-five and has a sexual relationship with a man in his sixties, who is also in another relationship. This would not have satisfied her in her youth – indeed, it would have been completely out of the question – but now, she says, she is happier than she has ever been. There is no need to end up sad and lonely, or slowly fossilising in a dead-end partnership. There are always more possibilities.

Some years ago, I was asked by Richard, who had come to one of my groups, to work with him and his wife. When they first married they adored each other. Now, ten years on, he was in despair, feeling that there was nothing left of his marriage except the outward form. His wife, Sarah, never wanted to make love, was tired all the time and seemed only to want him as a provider and to take the children off her hands when he was not working. He had just started an affair, and said that after all those years of marriage and drudgery he had found someone who could meet and enjoy his passion.

When Richard and Sarah first came to see me, they seemed to fit the picture he had painted. He was full of nervous energy and feeling, while she was drab, slow-moving, and said very little. I had the sense, however, that a great deal was hidden below the surface. Almost at the end of the session, having worked quite hard to bring her out, I remarked to Sarah that she had the potential to be a beautiful and dynamic woman. Richard laughed scornfully, while she looked at me as though she could not believe what she had heard.

Over the next few months I worked with them both together and separately, and I began to see a very different picture. Richard was angry with Sarah for not being what he wanted her to be, yet when she did shine, he missed it. She loved to sing, but her singing irritated him, so she had fallen silent. She enjoyed dancing, but he did not, and always wanted to leave early when they went to a party. Little by little, she had faded, until he had almost lost her.

Through therapy, Sarah began to regain her self-esteem and to enjoy herself again. Grudgingly at first, Richard learned to accept, and to respect, the woman to whom he was married; as he did so, their relationship, which had contracted almost to nothing, was able to expand. There was love between them underneath it all, and as they worked through some of the tangles they had got into, it began to grow. He came to understand that if he wanted her to meet his passion, he had also to learn to meet hers; and as I had glimpsed in that very first session, she had passion in plenty.

This is not a fairy story, and they certainly did not live happily ever after. Instead, they grew up. Growing up means seeing with clear eyes and accepting what you see. You may not like everything about each other, but if you can learn to let it be, then you make space for magic of a different kind. You can allow yourself and your partner to be more than you thought you were; you can play with possibilities. And from acceptance comes respect and affirmation. Not only can you allow each other to be what you are, but you can also help each other to expand. Being grown up means being able to be childish, to be silly and playful and passionate and sensible, and also to be wrong sometimes.

Steps to maturity

I can't give a recipe for a mature relationship, because I do not believe that there is ever a point at which we actually get there. At this stage in my life, I feel that I have arrived at a place – more or less! – beyond illusion and disillusion, where my relationship with my partner is nourishing to both of us. Where we go from here, I don't know. I strongly suspect that if we are still together when we are in our eighties, we will still sometimes hurt each other, and misunderstand each other, and get it wrong. My hope is that we will continue to get better at moving through these places, and that we may spend more time enjoying ourselves together.

However, even if there is no recipe to follow, there are ingredients that seem to be common to long-term relationships in which both partners are committed to becoming more alive and awake, rather than finding a comfortable pattern to settle into. One of them is disillusionment, as we have seen: the readiness to let go of what you thought you wanted and to embrace what is really there.

Along with disillusionment comes the knowledge that there cannot always be a perfect meeting between you and your partner. In other words, your truth may not be the same as their truth.

A good example of this was brought to me by my client Steve, whose girlfriend had come from Australia a few months ago to live with him and get married. He didn't feel sure about marriage, although he loved her and the relationship was going well. She became depressed, and was thinking of going back to Australia. In therapy he was able to hear and accept that for her it had to be marriage or nothing; that was the truth for her. It was not his truth, but he had to accept that it had validity for her and make his choice accordingly.

Another ingredient in long-term relationships is the acceptance of conflict and the willingness to work with it. This requires you to use and to refine all the skills at your command. It means being able to espouse your own position passionately and wholeheartedly, taking the risk of getting it wrong and losing face, and also being able to let go of that position, to move with the flow of the argument, towards resolution and new learning.

Again, the key here is that *both* partners must be willing. At any stage in a relationship, if one partner wants to explore new possibilities and the other does not, then the first partner is left with a choice: to accept the status quo, to leave, or to try to create an environment in which the other may choose to awaken. You can't change others, but you can, with love, invite them to change themselves.

Another ingredient is commitment, the vessel in which the relationship is held, which enables you to dive deep and to fly high. I could go on list making, but I have chosen to highlight the aspects of relationships that we are often unwilling to accept. There are many others, of course, which come more easily. At the root of them all is the willingness to meet, heart to heart, body to body, soul to soul; and for an intimate partnership, the heart-to-heart meeting is both the beginning and the end of the journey. From it, from the flow of love between two people, everything else arises. The opposite of love is not hatred, but indifference.

How can you find the courage, the fierce passion of the heart, to keep burning through all the tangles of hurt and misunderstanding and inertia that come between you, growing over the path and preventing this heart-to-heart meeting? The answer, as always, is to turn back to yourself, and to clear away the undergrowth that comes between you and your own heart's delight.

As children we all started out wide open and undefended. We were all born with the ability to reach for what we wanted and fight for it, able to rage and rejoice and be quietly happy. We all learned, as we grew, to defend ourselves from hurt, to resent and to manipulate and to feel unloved. And we all need to find our way back to the full spectrum of our feelings; we need to choose, and keep on choosing, to open up rather than shutting down, to follow the path of life rather than the path of death. Every time we make this choice, we allow ourselves a little more aliveness, a little more capacity for love; in so doing, we make ourselves a little more available for relationship.

Phases in relationships

It seems to me that there are three phases in intimate relationships.

1. ILLUSION

The first phase is that of illusion, of reaching out to another who seems to embody those extraordinary or magical qualities for which we yearn. Here is where romantic love belongs, and where many – though by no means all – partnerships begin.

2. CODEPENDENCE

The second phase is that of compromise. Still trying to make ourselves complete through partnership, we try to avoid the areas where we clash, and look to each other to fill up our holes. Contracts are drawn up, consciously or otherwise: you make me feel safe, not lonely, and I will provide for you. You do the feeling for both of us, and I will do the thinking. I love your sparkle; you love my solidity. We complement each other.

This phase, which is sometimes called codependence, is an inevitable part of partnership. It enables us to do what we cannot do on our own. On the practical level, for instance, it provides the conventional framework within which to start a family: the woman gives birth to and cares for the babies, while the man provides for them. However, unless we can also move beyond this phase, it becomes toxic, stifling our growth and holding us to patterns that keep us incomplete, unfulfilled. What starts out as a fair trade becomes set in stone; we 'give' certain qualities or roles to the other person in the partnership only to find that we cannot then have them for ourselves. If one partner seeks to change, the other is threatened and the equilibrium is lost.

> Nicki came to me because she had ME and wanted to do some work on herself as part of her journey of recovery. Later, she brought along her husband, Peter, as well. They presented themselves as a very modern couple, reversing the traditional roles. He did all the cleaning, shopping and cooking. The trouble was, he did everything else as well: he went out to work, managed their joint finances and 'looked after everything', including Nicki.

As Nicki had become ill, so he had taken on more and more, and he felt very good about being so caring and responsible. The story they told was of mutual support and satisfaction, but in reality she had ended up with no role and no sense of her own identity. This was fine until she began to recover, when the codependent structure they had built up became a prison from which she was unable to break free.

Together, we looked at ways in which they could begin to change things. She took on some household chores – nothing too strenuous or demanding at first, but it gave her a role to play and she began to feel happier. In turn, Peter had to give up being in control. After a difficult beginning, he came to realise that this freed him up to put energy into other things, interests he'd had no time for. With the change in responsibilities came a change in the fabric of the relationship; as Nicki became more of her own person and felt better about herself, she realised that she had been harbouring resentments against Peter. He in turn had felt hard done by and under-appreciated. Slowly, they began to move towards a more fluid and equal relationship.

The system lacks flexibility, and this tends to show up in times of crisis and change, when new strategies are needed. In the ordinary course of events, every partnership encounters some of these crises: the birth of children, illness, job changes or loss of work, attraction to others outside the partnership, looking after elderly relatives and death. These difficult times are invitations to take another step into maturity, to look within and to cultivate your own potential, your own resources.

3. MATURITY

Out of these hard times, when your coping mechanisms break down and the old structures fall apart, comes the third phase of relationship. As you allow yourself to feel your own pain and your own despair, and as you begin to take responsibility for your own healing, so you begin to release your partner and your friends from the old contracts.

It is not that you stop needing other people; on the contrary, the need for loving and truthful friends and companions is a theme that has come up again and again. What happens is that you stop needing them to complement you, to complete you. When you meet another person, you come to that meeting from a place of fullness, rather than emptiness. And if you do not need them to supply something that you lack, or to play some part in your movie, then you can allow them simply to be who they are. This, in itself, is profoundly transformative.

It will repay us to look at some of the crisis points in more detail, for each, in its own way, represents an invitation to try out a new way of being. The three that seem to me to hold the most potential are: having children, having affairs and the ending of the partnership through death. How can you respond to these invitations?

Having children

There are two main points here. One is the summons to grow up, to make yourself and all your resources available to a new and totally dependent being who, for a time at least, will dominate what was once a partnership. No one is ever ready for this, and not many of us can answer the summons wholeheartedly, however joyfully we welcome parenthood. As with other aspects of relationships, we learn on the job.

And it goes on, long past the first skills needed to care for a new baby. As the child grows, it requires you to cultivate patience, to slow down, to draw upon your creativity and your diplomacy, to withdraw your projections and fantasies and let it be its own self. A friend of mine had spent a lot of time and energy travelling around to hear the teachings of various spiritual masters. He said that when he came home to his wife and two-year-old son, it struck him with the force of revelation that his teaching had been right there, waiting for him all the time. If you can only find the courage and humility to let them take the lead, your children can teach you so much of what you need to know.

The second point is that, even as having children invites you to take a step into adulthood, it also invites you to rediscover your own inner child. Through your children's freshness and spontaneity, their wonder and delight, you can find your way back to your inner child. Through their ability to flow with their feelings, they remind you what you have lost, and show you what it means to be whole. For this teaching, too, you owe them your gratitude.

Having affairs

We have seen that a strong and healthy partnership exists at the centre of a many-stranded web of relationships. You need friends to challenge, support and nourish you. Intimacy is not exclusive; the more friends you have with whom you can open your heart, the easier it becomes, and the less satisfied you are with friendships that are not open-hearted. And yet, if you can be emotionally and spiritually intimate with others when you are in partnership, why can't you be physically intimate as well?

There are no easy answers here. What works for one couple may be disaster for another. For me, the touchstone has to be the love and respect at the core of the partnership. If being sexual with someone else means keeping secrets from your partner, then deception has come upon the scene, open-heartedness is no longer possible and energy is being taken out of the partnership. If, on the other hand, you can be as open about your sexual attractions or encounters as you can about any other kind of connection with others – and if you can stay open, dealing with whatever hurt or jealousy or confusion arises – this too can be a rich opportunity for the relationship to go deeper.

In his novel *The Magus*, John Fowles gives two simple rules for the successful handling of sexuality between partners: to tell no lies; and never to hurt one another more than is necessary. This allows for the fact that we do hurt one another whether we intend to or not, and leaves open the question of how much hurt is necessary. Only your own heart can give you the answer to that question.

159

Clare and Stefan have found their way to an open relationship that works for them. After fifteen years they are still together, bringing up their son, working together, growing and thriving. When the temptation to be unfaithful first arose a few years into their partnership, they talked about it and decided to try to explore it in a way that felt safe for them. Eventually, they engaged with another couple. They all agreed that if any one of them felt uncomfortable about what was happening at any time, they would stop.

There have been some difficult times along the way, but they have never broken faith with each other. What they discovered was a genuine delight in seeing each other making love with other people. It has enhanced their own sex life together, and completely removed the possibility of affairs, with their deceits and their undermining of relationship.

My own feeling is that, more often than not, you are drawn to make sexual connections outside an established partnership when you perceive a lack of something – sexuality, romance, adventure – within it. In other words, the affair arises from a place of hunger or emptiness. It may feed the hunger, but it also enables you to avoid looking at what is going on within the partnership. If you take your passion elsewhere, the vital energy at the heart of the partnership is bound to suffer. Once again, therefore, the temptation to be 'unfaithful' offers you the opportunity to wake up and to put your own house in order.

Until death us do part

It may sound nonsensical to speak of death as an opportunity to deepen a relationship. Certainly, when one partner dies suddenly and unexpectedly there is nothing to do but mourn. However, it is not so unusual to have some warning that death is approaching. A similar situation arises when a couple is facing a prolonged parting, for whatever reason.

The temptation is to try to tie up the loose ends, to 'make the most' of the time that is left. What this means is that, once again, all that is difficult or might lead to conflict must be suppressed. For the sake of a beautiful ending, we choose to withhold our truth. And what is so desperately sad is that in making this choice, we begin to die to each other long before the moment of death arrives. I have worked with many people who are dying or who are close to someone who is dying, and the loneliness that they have to bear in censoring what they say and what they feel can be heartbreaking to witness.

What would happen if, instead, we used this awareness of death or departure to sweep away the barriers between us? If, with nothing more to lose, we chose to be fully alive to one another? I worked with one couple who made this choice, and what I saw was that their relationship went through an astonishing process of transformation in a very short space of time.

John and Julie were in their forties and had been together for seven years. She was one of the most passionately alive people I have ever met, and when she suddenly discovered that she had a malignant brain tumour and would probably be dead within a year, her chief response was rage. She turned her anger upon John and upon anyone else who tried to get close to her. The only options for him were to withdraw or to weather the storm.

Up until this time, John and Julie had enjoyed some of the best things that partnership has to offer. They were financially comfortable, well matched physically and mentally, and still in love with each other. Theirs was a passionate, volatile relationship, and neither was afraid of conflict. In the past, however, Julie had tended to resolve conflict – or rather not resolve it – by leaving. Dramatic exits were her speciality.

Now, Julie could no longer do this. Instead, it was John who tried to take the edge off the intensity of the situation, using cigarettes and heavy drinking to dull his feelings. Julie would not let him get away with it. Fired by the knowledge that time was running out, she would have none of the kindness, the tactful avoidance of pain that is the usual lot of the terminally ill. She fought for her life, and she fought for the life of her relationship, in a process that was both painful and awe inspiring.

John stayed the course. Initially, he had done his best to support Julie in her search for healing, concealing the knowledge given to him by the doctors that it was hopeless. However, he came to feel that by withholding the truth he was doing Julie no favours. What mattered was the quality of the time they had left, rather than its quantity. Bracing himself to meet her fury, he gave her the full prognosis.

Julie's response was extraordinary. At some instinctive level, she knew that death was imminent. Once that knowledge was shared, she was able to stop fighting. Instead, she directed her formidable resources into the process of dying, embracing it with the same passion that she had brought to her life. Within a week or two, she was spending much of her time in a state of profound meditation. Visiting her felt like being in the presence of the Dalai Lama, and when I left, I took with me a sense of serenity and wonder that would last for some days. John describes walking along the beach with her, very slowly, simply being and observing, lost in reverence.

In those last few weeks, Julie healed her life. Together, she and John were able to transcend many of their old stumbling blocks, and their relationship came to maturity. They achieved a profound respect for each other that was a rare privilege to witness. This came about simply because, rather than living in denial of death, as we all do most of the time, they chose to embrace it, and to be open to all the new possibilities that this brought them. Along with the inevitable pain and sorrow, they found an amazing joy and grace, an intense aliveness that carried them far beyond their ordinary limits. Perhaps, if we were able to honour death as our constant travelling companion, we could find the courage to be fully alive.

Looking ahead

Is there any meaning in all this, beyond our own search for happiness? Do we undertake this work simply for our own sakes? I think not. I think that much of the struggle involved in learning to live with another is about fully embracing their reality, without losing our own. As we get better at this, it becomes less and less possible to try to control them, to abuse them, to make them play parts in our movie. We become free to meet, and to love, and to honour.

If we have children, the work takes on a new urgency, for we are their role models, and they will be the men and women who inherit the Earth. We do it for them, too. We do it for all of our companions on the road, for when one person takes a risk, or tries out a new way, it becomes a little easier for everyone else. And we do it for the Earth, our Mother. When we truly open ourselves to the reality of others, just as it becomes impossible to use and abuse the people around us, so it also becomes impossible to exploit and to cause needless destruction and pain to the Earth and to the other living beings with which we share our planet. In the true sense of the word, we become 'responsible'; able to respond, and to repay some of the energy that has been so freely invested in us.

This is no mystical vision. It is a highly practical one, for we on this small planet have to learn to live together somehow, for our lives' sake. It is here, in our own homes, with our own partners, that the learning begins. Through the day-to-day practice of truthful relationship, we can create a way of being that answers the needs of our times.

. . . Now on to the next thing

In this chapter we've had a look at the qualities that go to make up a mature relationship, and one that is likely to weather the storms. After all this, there is one last step to take. In the next and final chapter, we look at projecting your relationship into the future. Where will you go from here?

Chapter 9
Into the Future

If you and your partner have worked on developing the skills we have talked about, you have all the makings of a long-lasting relationship. However, there is one last skill – or technique, perhaps, would be a better word – that people often do not use at all. In the business world, from one-man operations to huge corporations, it is routine practice to look at forecasts, develop aims and objectives, and try to predict what circumstances may throw in your way. This means that you are ready and able to respond appropriately to changes as they come up. It also means more than this: that you are able to shape some of those changes for yourself, to take the initiative and create your own future. If you don't pay attention to the future, your business is very likely to fail.

All this is well understood. When it comes to relationships, however, we tend to be much less on the ball. The old 'happy ever after' myth still lingers on; once you are together, you can forget about maintaining your relationship. It will just muddle along, somehow, weathering all the blows. Plans for the future tend to be vague, as though your relationship comes at the bottom of the list when it comes to sorting out your priorities. Without being conscious of what we are doing, we tend to think along the lines of 'Well, of course, it depends on how work goes, whether we have children and what they are doing, where we live, how the family is', and so forth. In other words, your relationship has to react to everything else that goes on, and never gets to be the driving force.

When that happens to a person, they get depressed. What do you think it does for the health of your relationship? And yet, in all the research findings on what makes us happy and likely to live a long and healthy life, being in a relationship comes way above some of the other things we set such store by. It's more important than having money, and more important than having children. People who are in relationships live, on average, several years longer than those who are not. Surely something that is such a powerful force for good in our lives is worth looking after. Certainly, it deserves to be higher up on the list. Perhaps the future needs to be shaped around it, rather than the other way around. So try this exercise together with your partner, and see what it has to show you.

Exercise 23
Shaping your future

STEP 1

Sit down with your partner in your usual place. You are going to think about where you want this relationship to be in, say, five years' time. Choose the period of time that feels right to both of you. Each of you needs a pen and some paper; you will compare notes later, but for now, do the exercise separately.

Now imagine that you are there, five years from now. Create a picture of your relationship in as much detail as you can manage. Make sure that what you envisage is possible; that you and your partner could actually make it happen, if you chose to. Make sure that it is also desirable, that the changes are ones that will enrich your lives together.

Use these questions to help you:

What sort of home do you have? Do you live together or apart? Are you in the same town, or even the same country?

Do you have children? How many, how old? Who are they, and what sort of relationship do you have with them?

What about friends and family? What part do they play in your lives?

165

How is your health? How is your partner's health?

How is your sex life? Are you faithful to each other?

How well off do you feel financially? What is your work, and do you enjoy it?

What does a normal day look like?

What exciting experiences do you create together?

What do you do to nourish yourself, and each other?

STEP 2

From the perspective of the future relationship that you have just imagined, look back to where you are now, in the present. Ask yourself these questions:

What obstacles did we have to overcome in order to arrive at this vision of our future?

How did we do it?

STEP 3

Put aside what you have written for now. Each of you in turn will now talk about your vision for your shared future. As you talk, put your passion and your energy into it. Build your picture with colour and texture; put in details. This is not a business plan for your bank manager; it is a kind of proposal to your beloved, so make it glow.

As you listen, try not to think about what you are going to say when it is your turn. Don't dwell on the differences between your partner's vision and your own; those are inevitable, unless you are telepathic! Just listen, with an open heart. Your partner is giving you their hopes and dreams for the growth of your lives together. Notice if you feel cynical or disappointed at any point, but put those feelings aside. Notice where your enthusiasm does not meet your partner's, at those parts of their story you don't want to be a part of; you will talk about this later. Notice, especially, where your excitement rises as you listen, where you are surprised or touched or delighted. At the end, thank them.

STEP 4

Talk together about what has been said and how you are feeling. In particular, look at the areas where your visions overlap. Let's assume that there are some; otherwise, maybe your relationship is not as healthy as you thought! It is fine for one of you to have more energy for a particular aspect of the plan than the other, as long as there are core areas where your dreams coincide. Don't give too much weight to the bits that don't match, unless they are really central to one partner's vision and not the other's; having children would be an example of this. Look at what you both want to do together.

STEP 5

How are you going to make it happen? For now, choose one thread in the imaginary tapestry you have woven, and think about how to make it real. Be specific and definite; if you want it to happen within the next five years, you have to start from here. So, for example, if you want to build in more travelling together, arrange that one or both of you will collect information on holidays during the next week. If you want to move house, decide to contact estate agents. And so on.

Don't try to work on too many threads at once, but do make a commitment to review the plan next week or sometime soon. Keep the momentum going. If this works as it should, you will both gain a sense of fresh energy and excitement – and some of your visions, at least, may start to be realised sooner than you imagined.

At the end of the day

There never really is an end to any relationship. There will never be a point when you get there, when all the problems are sorted out and you achieve perfect intimacy. However, there will, if you are open-hearted and willing to take risks, be many, many moments of joy and beauty on your relationship journey. Plenty of people have looked back at the end of their lives and regretted their failures in relationships – but no one ever looked back and regretted making a relationship work. There is no job more worth doing. I wish you grace and courage on your journey, and may your dreams, after all, come true.

Index

If you enjoyed reading this book, you may be interested in the following Piatkus titles:

The Art of Sexual Magic
Margot Anand

Barefoot Doctor Handbook for Modern Lovers: A spiritual guide to truly rude and amazing love and sex
Barefoot Doctor

Becoming Orgasmic: A sexual and personal growth programme for women
Julia R. Heiman and Joseph LoPiccolo

Be Your Own Counsellor: A step-by-step guide to understanding yourself better
Sheila Dainow

The Big O: How to have them, give them, and keep them coming
Lou Paget

A Complete Guide to Love and Sex
Cassandra Eason

Creating Love
John Bradshaw

Dare to Connect
Dr Susan Jeffers

Difficult Conversations
Anne Dickson

The Gift of Therapy: Reflections on being a therapist
Dr Irvin Yalom

Heal Yourself: Simple steps to heal your emotions, mind and soul
Anne Jones

Hot Monogamy
Dr Patricia Love and Jo Robinson

How to Be a Great Lover
Lou Paget

How to Give Her Absolute Pleasure: Totally explicit techniques every woman wants her man to know
Lou Paget

If I'm So Wonderful, Why Am I Still Single?
Susan Page

If We're So in Love, Why Aren't We Happy?
Susan Page

Inner Happiness
Vera Peiffer

The Lazy Girl's Guide to Good Sex
Anita Naik

The Love Laws: 9 essential secrets for lasting, loving partnership
Steven Carter

Make Love Work for You
Anne Nicholls

What Men Want: Three single professional men reveal what it takes to make a man yours
Gerstman, Pizzo and Seldes

Women and Desire
Polly Young-Eisendrath

Women Who Think Too Much
Dr Susan Nolen-Hoeksema